Behavior Modification and Therapy

Behavior Modification and Therapy

An Introduction

Richard R. Bootzin
NORTHWESTERN UNIVERSITY

Winthrop Publishers, Inc.
CAMBRIDGE, MASSACHUSETTS

Library of Congress Cataloging in Publication Data

Bootzin, Richard R
  Behavior modification and therapy: an introduction,
mass., Winthrop Pub.
  Bibliography: p.   180p   23 cm
  Includes indexes.
  1. Behavior modification.   2. Behavior therapy.
I. Title.   [DNLM: 1. Behavior therapy. WM420
B725b]
BF637.B4B66   616.8'914   75-17801
ISBN 0-87626-063-6

ACKNOWLEDGMENTS

Fig. 2-1, p. 10: Copyright 1969 by the American Psychological Association. Reprinted by permission.
Fig. 2-3, p. 25: Copyright 1972 by the American Psychological Association. Reprinted by permission.
Fig. 3-1, p. 38: Copyright 1966 by the American Association for the Advancement of Science.
Table 3-1, pp. 50–51: Copyright 1965 by the Society for the Experimental Analysis of Behavior, Inc.
Fig. 3-5, p. 58: Copyright © 1964 by the Society for Research in Child Development, Inc. All rights reserved.
List, pp. 83-84: Copyright 1964 by the American Psychological Association. Reprinted by permission.
Fig. 4-5, p. 104: Copyright 1969 by the American Psychological Association. Reprinted by permission.
Excerpts, pp. 107 (bottom) and 108: Copyright 1970 by the American Psychological Association. Reprinted by permission.
Fig. 5-2, p. 122: Copyright 1969 by the American Psychological Association. Reprinted by permission.

© *1975 by Winthrop Publishers, Inc.*
17 Dunster Street, Cambridge, Massachusetts 02138

To Mitzi, Debbie, and Lainey, with love

Contents

Preface

This book is a broad introduction to the principles and techniques of behavior modification as applied to such diverse problem behaviors as overeating, fears, compulsions, hallucinations, classroom inattentiveness, and family discord. It is not intended as a handbook for therapists but as an overview of interest to everyone from the undergraduate psychology student to the informed layman.

Many students and colleagues have helped enormously in preparing this book. In particular, I would like to thank Len Sushinsky for his comments on the entire manuscript and Peter Herman for his suggestions on Chapter 6. I am grateful to Lyn Abramson, Barbara Lefsky, and Lee Schwartz for their efforts in preparing the glossary and index. Paul O'Connell and Barbara Sonnenschein at Winthrop Publishers have been delightful to work with and have made the last stages of putting the manuscript into print a pleasure.

I owe a special debt of gratitude to my wife, Mitzi, who has been my very active collaborator during every step of the process and who painstakingly tried to teach me how to write.

R. B.

1

What Is
Behavior Modification?

What indeed is behavior modification? In common parlance, the words *behavior modification* have been used to refer to almost any intervention intended to change behavior. In actuality, the term has a precise, technical definition. Behavior modification is *the attempt to apply learning and other experimentally derived psychological principles to problem behavior.*

The study of learning has always generated considerable interest within psychology, and the contributions of learning researchers have included practical applications for many aspects of life. For example, the application of learning principles has resulted in innovations such as programmed learning, and in improved techniques of animal training, job and skill training, and memorizing and studying. Recently, these learning principles have been used in a major effort to develop practical techniques for dealing with deviant behavior and personal problems including mental illness, aggressiveness, criminal behavior, fears, compulsions, obesity, and smoking. The result of this effort has been called behavior modification or behavior therapy. Although the term *behavior modification* is somewhat more general than the term *behavior therapy,* there is no clear distinction between the two. Both refer to the application of learning and other experimentally derived psychological principles to behavior change, and they can be used interchangeably.

From very cautious and hesitant beginnings, the development

1

of behavior modification techniques has resulted in a virtual revolution in the treatment of problem behavior within the past 15 years. But along with its increasing popularity behavior therapy has been burdened with increasing controversy. Some of this controversy is traceable to critics' misunderstanding of what behavior modification is. They tend to confuse behavior modification with procedures derived from clearly different conceptual frameworks. Techniques derived from a biological model (including drug treatments, psychosurgery, and electroconvulsive shock) are not behavior modification even though they may effectively change behavior.

The confusion results from an unhappy choice of labels to characterize the application of learning principles. The label has meaning, however. The word *behavior* was intended to emphasize the difference between behavior therapy procedures and traditional insight-oriented treatments. Traditional treatments usually rely upon the patients' understanding and insight into their own problems as the means for changing their subsequent behavior. In behavior therapy, insight is abandoned in favor of focusing on changing, or modifying, the problem behavior directly. But, again, and this cannot be repeated too often, not every means of changing behavior falls within the definition of behavior modification.

Another source of confusion results from what one author (Goldiamond, 1974) calls a failure to distinguish between analysis and control. Many aspects of human interaction can be analyzed using learning principles, but that does not make the people engaging in those interactions behavior modifiers. Thus, a mother praising her child is no more a behavior therapist than a child flying a kite is an applied physicist. Although the effectiveness of psychoanalysis, sensitivity groups, tortures, and bribes could all be analyzed using learning principles, that does not make them behavior modification techniques, nor their users behavior therapists.

Not all of the behavior modification controversy is due to mislabeling or misunderstanding. Some serious ethical questions have been raised by the use of certain techniques in particular settings. These questions will be discussed in subsequent chapters as the techniques are described. More general questions about ethics and about the philosophical view of humanity that is implied by a behavioral orientation will be discussed in the final chapter.

What indeed is behavior modification? It is the attempt to apply primarily learning principles, but also other experimentally derived psychological principles, to problem behavior. It focuses on observable behavior and requires a concrete description of the problem to be changed. A treatment is considered effective to the extent to which that problem behavior is altered.

Another, and very important, characteristic of behavior modification is a continuing emphasis on evaluation. Although certain techniques may have been suggested by positive results in the laboratory, behavior therapists have been cautious about applying them without a concurrent evaluation of their effectiveness. For some behavior therapists, this process of evaluation and confirmation is the hallmark of behavior modification; to them, the experimental methodology is the most important contribution behavior therapists have made to clinical endeavors.

Are Problem Behaviors Symptoms?

Traditional psychotherapists (particularly psychoanalysts) have warned against direct treatment of problem behavior. In their view, problem behavior is usually a symptom of some underlying personality disorder. If the symptom is changed without attacking the underlying disorder, traditionalists expect symptom substitution. For example, a traditionalist may consider fear of heights to be a sign of dependency caused by unresolved childhood conflicts. From that point of view, it would follow that if the fear (the symptom) is treated successfully while the underlying conflicts remain, a new symptom (perhaps fear of being alone) will replace the old one.

On the surface, it appears the question of symptom substitution is empirical—one for which we should be able to collect evidence one way or the other. However, the warnings of traditional therapists had discouraged people for years from treating problem behavior directly, so there was little evidence available for evaluation. In addition, the question is stated in a way that makes it almost impossible to investigate. In the normal course of events a person's behavior constantly is changing. After treatment has been administered, which changes should we count as substitutions and which should we count as normal changes? How long should we wait before deciding that there was no symptom substitution? 1 month? 6 months? 2 years? 5 years? 10 years?

Although the question of symptom substitution can never be answered with complete satisfaction, it is possible to ask whether direct treatment of one set of behaviors affects other behaviors within a specific time span. In other words, at the end of direct treatment for one specific fear, is the treated person more or less afraid in other situations? Phrased in this way, data are available for those problem behaviors treated by behavior therapists. In brief, investigators have consistently found that other aspects of a person's adjustment improve rather than get worse after direct treatment. This really should not be surprising. Improvement, even in a very focused problem, is bound to affect other aspects of life. Some problems put considerable strain on personal relationships. A woman who is afraid to be out of her house alone may be a burden to those around her. However, if that woman receives an effective treatment and is more comfortable being out alone, her demands on those around her will lessen and her relationships likely improve. This in turn may lead to other positive changes in her life.

The very use of the phrase *symptom substitution* implies belief in an underlying disorder. Actually, we know only that a person is having difficulties in particular situations. Not all problem behaviors indicate deep-seated disease processes. Many such behaviors are learned. Consequently, the same principles that apply to behaviors considered normal may also apply to problem behaviors.

There have been experimental tests of the hypothesis that deviant behaviors can be learned. One is the famous demonstration conducted over a half-century ago by John B. Watson and Rosalie Rayner (1920). Watson and Rayner were reluctant to perform the experiment but felt it was very important to discover whether fears could be learned. Their subject was Albert, an 11-month-old baby who was quite placid and seldom cried. Albert was so well adjusted they felt reassured that no lasting harmful effects would be produced by the experiment. The neutral stimulus was a white rat with which Albert had played for weeks. Before the study, the experimenters had noticed that a loud noise produced a startle and fear reaction in the baby. They decided to condition Albert to fear the rat by pairing the rat with the already-feared sound.

For the first conditioning trial, a three-foot-long steel bar was struck with a hammer behind Albert just after he had reached out and touched the rat. Albert was startled but did not cry. This loud noise was paired with the presence of the rat once more that day and five more times seven days later. Then the rat was presented without the noise. The laboratory notes for that trial state:

> The instant the rat was shown, the baby began to cry. Almost instantly he turned sharply to the left, fell over on left side, raised himself on all fours and began to crawl away so rapidly that he was caught with difficulty before reaching the edge of the table (Watson and Rayner, 1920, p. 5).

Six days later, Albert still showed fear of the rat. In addition, he cried and whimpered at the sight of animals and objects of which he had not been afraid before conditioning (a rabbit, a dog, a sealskin coat, and a Santa Claus mask). He avoided touching a package of wool but did not show a marked fear reaction. Albert showed no negative reaction to blocks, paper, or the experimental room and its furniture. Thus, Albert's fear had generalized to some related objects but not to others.

Although this is a convincing demonstration that fear can be conditioned, it does not demonstrate that all, or even most, fears are conditioned. For a behavior modifier to state categorically that all fears are learned would be as speculative as for a traditionalist to attribute all fears to personality conflicts. Yet, there is an important advantage to using such a hypothetical model of how deviant behavior develops, for it suggests ways of modifying behavior. The Watson and Rayner study demonstrates that fears can be learned, and thus suggests that fears might also be unlearned using the same principles.

Even when there is an underlying personality disorder, improvement might still be produced through the application of learning principles. For example, there is little debate that certain types of mental retardation have genetic or biological causes. Nevertheless, it is possible to increase significantly the degree of learning and adaptability of retardates by means of behavior modification procedures. A biological cause does not imply a need for a biological treatment. By the same token, improvement by means of behavior modification does not necessarily indicate that the problem originated from faulty learning.

Behavior therapy focuses on how the person is behaving—

now, in the present—not on how the problem originated. The following chapters document the fruitfulness of this approach.

Recommended Readings

Two sources which provide excellent introductions to behavior modification are:

BANDURA, A. *Principles of behavior modification.* New York: Holt, Rinehart and Winston, 1969. Chaps. 1 and 2.
ULLMANN, L. P., & KRASNER, L. *Case studies in behavior modification.* New York: Holt, Rinehart and Winston, 1965. Pp. 1–65.

2

Basic Principles

Everyone has habits and behaviors which he or she has at some time or another tried to change. These include giving up smoking, going on a diet, increasing studying, stopping from biting nails, and overcoming childhood fears. In this chapter, basic principles of behavior change will be introduced, using examples from attempts to change such common, everyday problems. The application of these principles to more severe behavioral disorders will be dealt with in detail in Chapters 3, 4, and 5.

Behavioral Assessment and Self-monitoring

FUNCTIONAL ANALYSIS

The first step in any behavior change program is to make a careful assessment of the frequency of the activity to be altered, the situations in which it occurs, and the consequences which follow it. This is called a *functional analysis*. It is an attempt to discover causal relationships between environmental events and the response of interest.

A person who is giving up smoking would take the first step of counting the number of cigarettes smoked each day and noting the time each one is taken and the situation (i.e., companions, activities being engaged in, and location). Some people discover that they only smoke when they are with someone else and never alone; other people discover that they smoke most frequently while driving and least frequently while working. It becomes obvious that smoking is not a continuous activity but rather occurs in the presence of certain environmental stimuli. Thus, the individual has already exerted some control—he does not smoke in some situations but finds it very difficult to refrain from smoking in others. A treatment strategy might then be a means of enabling him to extend the areas in which there already is good control to include areas in which he finds it difficult not to smoke.

In carrying out a functional analysis, accuracy is important. Although it might be possible, days later, to remember when a response occurred and what the consequences were, a functional analysis which depends upon remembered data is usually incomplete and often inaccurate. For example, parents who seek help for an aggressive child may overestimate considerably the frequency of aggressive behavior. Each new incident reinforces their view of the child as aggressive even if the incidents occur infrequently. They remember the aggressive behavior and discount or forget occasions when the child was not aggressive. Unless aggressive behavior is recorded as it occurs, information about the extent and tractability of the problem can be considerably biased. Another advantage of continuous monitoring of the problem behavior is that it will provide a means of evaluating later interventions.

SELF-MONITORING

For the purpose of providing accurate information, direct observation by an observer is always advantageous and sometimes essential. Persons monitoring their own behavior may present themselves in what they consider a socially acceptable light, whereas an observer would be relatively free of this bias. In addition, an observer might spot certain consistent stimuli or consequences that a directly involved person might not see.

Frequently, however, direct observation is impractical or expensive. Self-monitoring, under most circumstances, is an acceptable compromise. Most clients try to cooperate with a request for accuracy and are not likely to deceive the therapist intentionally. Unintentional biases can be reduced by making the client's task specific and unambiguous. Daily logs of a specific problem behavior would be less biased than statements obtained in an interview about the remembered frequency of the behavior.

The careful monitoring of one's own behavior often pays an additional dividend. By so doing some people change their behavior without any other treatments. For example, a friend of mine discovered that he was interspersing the phrase "you know" in almost every sentence he spoke. He decided to try to suppress that behavior. The first step that he took—as it turned out, the only step that was required—was to record the number of times that he said "you know." Each day that he recorded, his frequency of emitting that phrase decreased. Recording served as a sufficient intervention to bring that verbal behavior under control. His experience is not an unusual one. In most behavior modification programs, a baseline period is taken in which recording and nothing else is administered. The treatment is not started until it is clear that recording by itself will not be enough to alter the behavior completely.

A rather dramatic use of this principle was reported by Ivan Rutner and Charles Bugle (1969). They asked a hospitalized mental patient to use this self-monitoring procedure for her hallucinations. The patient (Eva) had been hospitalized for 13 years and throughout that period of time had reported that much of her behavior was controlled by "voices." Eva was asked to record privately the frequency of her hallucinations for a three-day period. During these three days the number of her hallucinations changed from 180 on the first day to 80 on the second day to about 10 on the third day (Figure 2-1). In order to maintain these remarkable gains, the record-keeping operation was made public. A chart was placed in full view of the ward personnel to indicate how many times each day Eva reported hearing voices. If she reported hearing them fewer times than she had on the previous day, she was praised and encouraged by the staff. This combination of public recording and contingent praise served to maintain her hallucinations at a near-zero frequency for the next two weeks. At this point, record keeping stopped because it was unnecessary. Eva did not have any recurrences of reported hallucination during six months subsequent to this treatment.

The question can be raised whether Eva stopped hallucinating or merely stopped reporting hallucinations. All we know def-

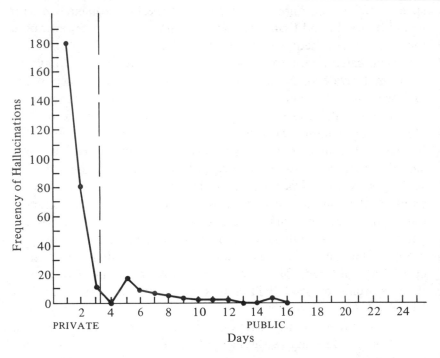

Figure 2-1
The daily frequency of Eva's reported hallucinations. (Adapted from Rutner and Bugle, 1969.)

initely is that she stopped reporting hallucinations, not whether she actually stopped hallucinating. If she had not reported or been concerned about her voices, there would be no way to verify that she had them. This suggests a number of possible outcomes.

One possibility assumes that her verbal reports accurately reflect whether she is experiencing unusual perceptual events. If we accept her word when she says that she is hallucinating, we ought to accept her word when she says she is not. The second possibility is that her original difficulty was the development of bizarre verbal behavior (*saying* she heard voices, not actually hearing them). These bizarre statements could have been maintained by the reinforcement she received from staff members interested in such reports. If this were the case, altering her verbal behavior, in fact, did solve her problem.

What about the remaining possibility that originally her verbal reports were accurate but for some reason she later said she was not hallucinating when she was? It seems unlikely that for six months she would give no indication to any staff member that she was still distressed when for the previous 13 years she had been quite open about this problem. Yet, what if that were the case? Even here, the change in her behavior is not trivial and would probably be therapeutic. Other people would no longer label her as deviant because of her "voices." She would be a different stimulus to them and they would react differently toward her. Finally, it would now be possible for staff members to help her plan for other more adaptive changes, since they would not be preoccupied with talking about her voices.

In the previous chapter we mentioned that bizarre and problem behavior is often taken as an indication of some underlying problem and that if it were treated directly there would be some danger of symptom substitution. In this case, hallucinations were treated as problems in themselves and the treatment was the very simple one of having Eva record the number of times she hallucinated. What else happened to her behavior? Did she get worse? Were there other symptoms? Or did the treatment of this symptom enable her to improve in other areas of functioning?

According to Rutner and Bugle:

> Concomitant with this reduction in reported hallucinations, a dramatic change was noted in other aspects of Eva's behavior. She appeared more relaxed, began to socialize more with other patients, her appearance improved, and she asked for a job. Perhaps more important, although less quantifiable, she appeared to be happier (Rutner and Bugle, 1969, p. 652).

Why does self-monitoring change behavior? One possibility is that it increases awareness and makes the response sequence less automatic. This may provide the opportunity for the person to suppress the response or engage in some incompatible behavior. Additionally, self-monitoring may encourage the person to reward or punish himself depending upon whether appropriate gains have been made. Investigators have shown that self-reinforcing statements such as "I am doing well" are important in maintaining one's own behavior. A recording system which facilitates this process undoubtedly will be effective in helping people to change their own behavior as well.

Another possibility is that it is not self-monitoring alone which is responsible for dramatic changes such as those described in the case of Eva. Although there is no question that the number of reported hallucinations decreased while Eva was recording, Eva may have improved initially in order to gain her therapist's approval. The self-monitoring data may have been only the documentation of her improvement. In a case study such as this, it is not possible to evaluate alternative hypotheses. Even in many experimental investigations of self-monitoring, some uncontrolled variable, such as the therapist's attention, may have been responsible for the observed changes (see Kazdin, 1974, for a review of this literature).

Nevertheless, self-monitoring would be expected to have an important role in self-control endeavors because, as Fredrick Kanfer and Jeanne Phillips (1970) point out, being able to observe one's actions with some objectivity is a prerequisite to being able to systematically change one's behavior.

Contingency Management

Contingency management refers to the process of changing the frequency of a response by controlling the consequences of that response. For example, to condition a rat to press a bar, food is delivered only after the rat makes the correct response. The experimenter arranges the consequences (delivery of food) in order to increase the frequency of the response (bar pressing). Any attempt to change the frequency of a response by systematically altering consequences is contingency management. Not only experts, but all of us are contingency managers. The boss giving a bonus, the mother punishing or rewarding her child, the boy telling his girlfriend how great she looks, are all trying to encourage or discourage particular behaviors by associating a consequence with them that is desirable or undesirable.

POSITIVE REINFORCEMENT

One type of contingency management is positive reinforcement. The most widely accepted definition of a positive reinforcer is *a stimulus which increases the frequency of the response it fol-*

lows. Thus, food is a positive reinforcer for the rat if its presentation increases the probability that the rat will press the bar.

How can we identify which stimuli will be reinforcing? The only sure way is to pair a stimulus with a particular response and observe whether or not the frequency of that response increases. Other attempts to identify reinforcers independently of the person and the situation have generally been unsatisfactory because there are always exceptions. For example, it was once thought that a stimulus was reinforcing if it satisfied a physiological need of the organism. We *need* food to live, and if we have been deprived of it, food usually functions as a reinforcer. However, we also need oxygen, and if slowly deprived of it, we fall unconscious, completely unaware of the deprivation.

Even the statement that food is reinforcing must be qualified. Food for one person is not food for another. Some people would not eat human flesh even if starving, others would. Taking a more mundane example, some people adore sweets, others can't stand them. Also, individuals often change their food preferences. For example, it is frequently said that you must learn to like scotch, olives, and pizza. Thus, a bottle of scotch may be very reinforcing when previously it had not been. Finally, the strength of a reinforcer varies with the amount of deprivation the organism has experienced. Ten minutes after a large dinner, food is not likely to be as reinforcing as it would be if the person had not eaten for a few hours.

One method of identifying reinforcing events has been suggested by David Premack (1965). He states that any high-probability behavior can be used to reinforce a low-probability behavior. If you give a *hungry* animal the choice of eating or running, it is likely to eat. Eating, then, is the high-probability behavior in that situation. If you used eating as the reinforcement for running, you could increase the frequency with which the animal engaged in running. Premack also showed that the reverse would hold. If an animal is deprived of the opportunity to run and allowed free access to food, running becomes the high-probability response. It then can be used to reinforce eating.

The Premack Principle has a number of practical advantages. It allows us to identify reinforcing events just by watching what the person does. If the individual prefers to watch television, watching television is reinforcing; if the individual prefers to eat ice cream, eating ice cream is reinforcing. Activities the person prefers are taken as reinforcing and may be used to increase the frequency of responses which the person otherwise would be unlikely to engage in.

There are many opportunities to use the Premack Principle in changing one's own behavior. For example, before starting to study, many students engage in all the activities they would prefer doing instead. They may read the newspaper, or have a Coke, or write a letter. These behaviors are higher-probability responses than is studying. To increase the frequency of studying, they should reverse the order; they should reinforce studying with newspaper reading. "After I have studied for 30 minutes, I'll read the newspaper." The same technique can be used to schedule assignments in more than one subject. If studying history is preferable to English, studying history can be made contingent upon the completion of the English assignment. The possibilities are endless.

Although the delivery of reinforcement appears to be an easy and straightforward procedure, many people fail at attempts to apply it to their own behavior. Of the factors which may contribute to failure, a primary one is setting the criterion for reinforcement too high. For example, someone who is unable to study at all may first need to reinforce himself for sitting at the desk, opening the book, and doing nothing more. The next time the student might reinforce himself for reading one page—then two, five, and so on. If the first criterion for self-reinforcement had been set at 25 pages, it might never have been reached, and the student might never have been reinforced. The process of reinforcing small bits of improvement is analogous to *shaping* a complex response by reinforcing *successive approximations* to it. In either case it is essential that the person have a high probability of receiving reinforcement at each step along the way.

There are some reinforcements which can only be delivered once and cannot be dispensed in small parcels for successive approximations to the final response. A night out on the town might be one such example. It would be too expensive and impractical to give yourself such a reinforcement for reading one page, then two pages, and so forth. Yet, it is often essential that reinforcement be delivered at each step along the way, not just for the final product. The best solution for this is to use *conditioned reinforcers*.

These are stimuli which have been associated with and signal the future delivery of other reinforcers. Money is a good example of this. It is exchangeable for a wide range of reinforcers. Thus, we could reinforce improvement in studying with small amounts of money which could accumulate and be used sometime later for a night out on the town. Other stimuli such as points or poker chips can also be used as conditioned reinforcers. They, too, can be accumulated and later exchanged for a back-up reinforcer. Besides permitting reinforcement of small increments of improvement, tangible conditioned reinforcers have additional advantages. They provide a visible record of improvement, they can be dispensed immediately after an appropriate response, and their value does not depend upon the deprivation or satiation associated with any one back-up reinforcer.

NEGATIVE REINFORCEMENT

Reinforcement always involves an event which increases the frequency of the response it follows. Negative reinforcement is the process in which the *omission or termination* of a stimulus increases the frequency of the preceding response. For example, a student may study immediately before an exam to avoid receiving an *F*. The student is reinforced for studying if he in fact avoids failing.

The avoidance of aversive events can also be used in changing one's own behavior. An interesting demonstration of this was performed by Rogers Elliott and Thomas Tighe (1968) with habitual smokers. Each subject gave the experimenters $65 which would gradually be returned if they abstained from smoking, but which they would lose as soon as they started to smoke. If a subject did not smoke for the first two days, $10 was returned to him; if the subject abstained for two weeks, another $10 was returned. By the end of the three-month program, a subject could earn back the entire $65. Each subject could avoid the aversive consequence of losing money by abstaining from smoking. At the same time, he was being reinforced for longer and longer periods of abstinence by the gradual return of the money. Of the 25 subjects who started, 21 remained abstinent throughout the entire program. At the end of a long-term follow-up, approximately 40 percent were still abstinent. These results are remarkable considering that each subject had to rely upon his own means of behavioral control when confronted with the urge to smoke. The threat of losing money was a powerful means to help maintain the subjects' motivation.

PUNISHMENT

Although punishment usually involves the application of unpleasant consequences, it is not defined in this way. A punishing stimulus is *any stimulus which decreases the frequency of the response it follows*. Thus, both punishment and reinforcement are defined solely by changes in response frequency. In fact, not all punishing stimuli are unpleasant or painful. For example, self-monitoring could be viewed as punishment in those instances in which it decreases the frequency of problem behavior. In addition, apparently aversive events are sometimes reinforcing rather than punishing. For example, a teacher's disapproval of disruptive behavior in the classroom may *increase* its frequency rather than decrease it. Thus, while the teacher may yell at children with the hope of punishing the behavior (i.e., decreasing its frequency), in reality he or she may be reinforcing it. To avoid such confusions between apparently aversive events and punishment, it is best to remember that punishment is defined independently of whether the consequence appears to be aversive. Only stimuli which decrease the frequency of the preceding target response are punishing stimuli.

A rather unusual example of punishment is a procedure suggested by Joseph Wolpe (1969) for suppressing obsessive thinking. All of us at some time or another have spent a sleepless night worrying about something (for example, an examination the next day or some financial problem). Although we may have recognized that worrying about it would not help, there seemed to be no way to suppress that behavior. Wolpe suggested the rather simple procedure of yelling "stop" to oneself (even just thinking "stop") as soon as the thought occurs. Yelling "stop" momentarily disrupts the problem thought and, if repeatedly paired with the thought, decreases its frequency.

Even imagined punishment seems to be effective. Joseph Cautela (1967) had overweight subjects imagine themselves eating some forbidden food (for example, a between-meal snack) and then imagine themselves becoming nauseated and vomiting. Thus, a punishment (nausea) was associated with the act of eating. Both the eating and the nausea were imagined. In addition to the imagined punishment trials, subjects would also imagine a number of reinforcement trials. They would imagine themselves about to eat something forbidden, refusing it, and then feeling better, comfortable, and pleased. Cautela reported that if subjects continued to use this imagined punishment and reinforcement system, their actual behavior was altered.

A systematic attempt to use punishment with smokers has been reported by J. Powell and Nathan Azrin (1968). Their experience illustrates a number of problems that may occur when using punishment. They constructed a special cigarette case which would deliver an electric shock to the subject's arm whenever the case was opened. They asked 20 male cigarette smokers (all over 21 years old) to volunteer for their experiment. Fourteen refused outright —many of them stating that they would rather continue smoking than go through a treatment involving electric shocks. Three more quit by the end of the first day. Only three subjects remained in the study. One obvious problem when using a painful punishment is keeping the subjects in the program.

Another way to escape the contingencies was not to wear the shock apparatus. The number of hours subjects wore the apparatus was a function of the intensity of the shock. The more intense the shock, the fewer hours the apparatus was worn. The effectiveness of the punishment also varied with intensity of shock. The more intense the shock, the fewer cigarettes taken. Thus, an intense shock suppressed smoking, but the subject exposed himself to that contingency for very few hours of the day. As soon as the punishment contingency was removed entirely, all three subjects returned to their original smoking rate.

There is a marked contrast between the Elliott and Tighe (1968) and the Powell and Azrin (1968) studies. One of the reasons the Elliott and Tighe program was successful was that the aversive consequences could not be escaped by terminating treatment. The $65 had been collected in advance and would be forfeited by either termination or the resumption of smoking. In addition, Elliott and Tighe's subjects were completely abstinent for the three months of the experiment. The subjects could not have the contingencies apply to just part of the day or escape them by reducing their smoking only slightly.

RESPONSE COST

Just as there are two kinds of reinforcement (positive and negative), so there are two kinds of punishment. Both types of reinforcement were defined as involving events which *increase* the frequency of the response they follow. Similarly, both types of punishment are defined as involving events which *decrease* the frequency of the response they follow.

Response cost produces a decrease in the frequency of the preceding response because a stimulus is omitted or terminated. Thus, fines, penalties, and the revocation of privileges are all instances of response cost. The frequency of the target responses is still decreased, but not because a stimulus is presented, but because a stimulus is removed. It is called response cost to indicate that the person "pays a price" for the behavior.

One of the first demonstrations of the potential of response cost was reported by Donald Baer (1962) for the problem of thumbsucking in children. He demonstrated that the frequency of thumbsucking could be decreased while a child watched cartoons by having the picture go off every time the child started thumbsucking. The "price" of thumbsucking was that there was no more picture. As long as the child kept his thumb out of his mouth, he could watch the cartoons uninterrupted.

Stimulus Control

When a response is reinforced only in the presence of particular cues, an animal quickly learns to emit that response only when the cues for reinforcement are present. These cues are called *discriminative stimuli*. For example, in a learning laboratory, a rat could be taught to barpress only when a light is on if barpresses are reinforced with food when the light is on and not reinforced when the light is off. Barpressing would then be under the "control" of the light. In other words, the light would be a highly valid predictor of whether the response would occur or not.

Overeating. Problem behavior, too, is under the "control" of discriminative stimuli. It occurs more frequently in some situations than in others. For example, watching television is a stimulus for eating for many people. As soon as they sit down in front of a television set, they start to eat. Such habits may become very persistent because the enjoyment of watching television reinforces eating. One possible treatment for overeating, then, would be to reduce the number of discriminative stimuli for eating. A number of ways for doing this have been suggested by Charles Ferster, John Nurnberger, and Eugene Levitt (1962):

First, eating could be made a pure experience. A person wanting to eat could do so if he did not engage in some other activity at the same time which might inadvertently reinforce eating. Thus, eating could not be paired with reading, watching television, listening to music, talking, and so forth. People can easily follow this instruction because food deprivation is not required. A person wanting an ice cream sundae may have one. The only restriction is that he not engage in any other activity at the same time.

Second, the discriminative stimuli for eating should not be discriminative stimuli for other activities. If a person both eats and studies in the kitchen, the kitchen is a discriminative stimulus for both activities, even if they are engaged in separately. In this case there are bound to be occasions when a person goes into the kitchen intending to study, but ends up eating. This will be a particular problem when studying is somewhat aversive and the person is seeking ways to avoid getting to work. The solution to this type of problem is to keep the stimuli for eating separate from stimuli for other activities. Eating should occur in a place in the house which is away from routine activities. The fewer times one finds himself where he ordinarily eats, the less he will eat. Similarly, stimuli characterizing the eating occasions should be made as unique as possible. People can be encouraged to use their imaginations to make an unusual eating ritual. Thus, a person might eat only when there is a purple table cloth on the table or only when he wears a particular item of clothing.

Richard Stuart (1967) developed a comprehensive and effective program for weight reduction relying heavily upon the stimulus control techniques proposed by Ferster, Nurnberger, and Levitt. Stuart's "behavioral curriculum," as he called it, will be described in detail to illustrate how different techniques can be used within one program.

First, subjects were asked to record "the time, nature, quantity, and circumstance of all food and drink intake" (p. 358). They were also asked to weigh themselves four times each day—before breakfast, after breakfast, after lunch, and before bedtime. These recording activities were to take place throughout the entire program, and were intended to help subjects develop a weight control language.

Step one of the behavioral curriculum was the instruction to interrupt each meal for two or three minutes and then gradually increase the interruption to five minutes. During this interval, subjects were to put down their utensils and just sit at the table for that period of time. Thus the first step, which involved increasing the chain of responses during the meal, was deliberately made easy to ensure that the subjects would experience success.

After the subjects had practiced step one, they were told to remove all food from places other than the kitchen (step two). In addition, they were instructed to keep in the house only foods that required preparation, except salad greens. When they prepared food, they were to prepare only one portion at a time.

Step three was to make eating a pure experience by engaging in no other activity while eating. Steps two and three, then, were to give subjects practice in using stimulus control principles.

After the subjects had become adept at these procedures, step four required them to slow down their rate of eating by placing only a small amount of food in their mouths at a time and to place their utensils back on the table until they had swallowed.

Step five required subjects to engage in a previously identified high-probability behavior at times when they would ordinarily eat. Before engaging in this behavior, subjects were instructed to repeat the phrase: "I can control my eating by engaging in other activities which I enjoy."

The last step (step six) of the program was to teach subjects to use covert sensitization for foods they had particular difficulty controlling. For example, if a subject could not resist cookies, she would repeatedly imagine becoming nauseated after eating them. (See Chapter 5 for a more complete description of this technique.)

The remarkable results of Stuart's program are presented in Figure 2-2. Particularly noteworthy is that this program took place

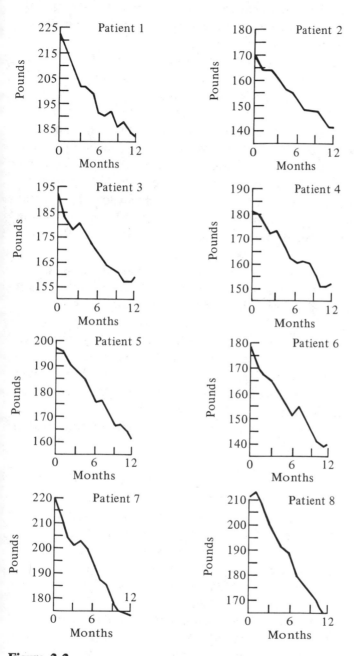

Figure 2-2
Weight profile of eight women undergoing behavior therapy for overeating. (From Stuart, 1967.)

over a period of 12 months and the subjects were still participating. Thus, Stuart had successfully shaped eating behaviors so that weight loss could be maintained over a long period of time.

Subsequently, in the process of working with over two hundred overweight women, Richard Stuart and Barbara Davis (1972) expanded the behavioral curriculum so that the procedures could be tailored to individual family requirements. The researchers discovered that it was essential to include other family members in the planning and execution of the program. In fact, the cooperation of family members would often determine whether the weight reduction program would be successful. Of the women who had the assistance of at least one other person, 83 percent lost 20 percent or more of their body weight. In contrast, only 31 percent of the women who could not depend on the cooperation of another person were this successful.

Although the Stuart and Davis program was effective, it was not an evaluation of stimulus control per se. Rather, theirs was a complex program and stimulus control techniques were only a part of it. A more focused evaluation was carried out by Michael Mahoney, Nanci Moura, and Terry Wade (1973). They compared the relative effectiveness of stimulus control, self-monitoring, self-reward, and self-punishment as treatments of obesity. They found that self-reward was the most effective of these self-help techniques. Nevertheless, the dramatic success described by Stuart and Davis indicates that stimulus control techniques have a secure place within comprehensive programs.

Studying. Overeating is an activity which is immediately reinforcing and for which the aversive consequences are delayed. Because eating is immediately reinforcing, it tends to become associated with a wide range of stimuli. As already described, a treatment based upon stimulus control attempts to reduce the number of discriminative stimuli as a way of reducing the frequency of the behavior. There are other problem behaviors for which the goal is *increasing* the frequency of the behavior (e.g., studying). Here the problem is that other activities associated with the same cues as studying interfere with studying. A stimulus control treatment would be possible with this type of problem as well.

An interesting example of a behavior change program for

studying using the principle of stimulus control was described by Israel Goldiamond (1965). He helped a young woman bring studying under the stimulus control of her desk. If she wished to write a letter, read comic books, or daydream, she was required to do those activities some place other than her desk; ". . . at her desk she was to engage in her school work and her school work only" (p. 854). She could spend as little time as she wished at her desk; however, when she was at her desk she was to study and do nothing else. After the first week of following these instructions she reported that she had spent only 10 minutes at her desk. However, she had spent that time studying. By the end of the semester, she was able to spend three hours a day at her desk for four weeks in a row, something she had been unable to do previously.

At the beginning of the program, she expressed reluctance at having the desk have stimulus control over studying. "I'm not going to let any piece of wood run my life for me," she said. Goldiamond's reply to her is worth repeating: "On the contrary, you *want* that desk to run you. It is you who decides when to put yourself under the control of the desk. It is like having a sharpened knife in a drawer. You decide when to use it, but when you want it, it is ready" (p. 117).

Insomnia. Insomnia is another problem area which might be alleviated by stimulus control procedures. The usual treatment for sleeping difficulties is sleeping pills. However, medication is often unsatisfactory since it does not help the person with chronic sleep problems develop new sleeping habits. In fact, the taking of pills may become a discriminative stimulus for sleep. A man may discover that he can sleep only after taking a pill; if he doesn't take a pill he doesn't sleep.

Sleeping difficulties not caused by illness are usually seen as the symptom of some other psychological problem. Thus, insomniacs are often recommended for psychotherapy with the reasoning that if their other more basic problems are resolved, they will also be able to sleep better. There is considerable intuitive appeal to this assumption since people who ordinarily have no trouble sleeping often develop insomnia during periods of stress. Insomnia, however, usually contributes to the worsening of the problem. Inability to sleep reduces the ability of the person to handle the very stress causing the insomnia. This can easily turn into a vicious cycle in which the person rapidly deteriorates.

However, it may be possible to intervene in this cycle by treating the insomnia directly and independently of the stress. In fact, this may be required for chronic insomniacs since their sleeping problems have persisted for so long that the insomnia is likely to be independent of situational stresses. But even when insomnia is associated with stress, alteration of the sleep problem may be possible without changing the reaction to stress. A person who stays awake because of worrying has learned to use bedtime as an occasion for worrying. It ought to be possible to make going to bed the occasion for sleeping (not worrying) without changing either the amount of or reason for worrying.

An opportunity arose to test whether a stimulus control treatment would be effective for someone complaining of insomnia (Bootzin, 1972). The subject was a 25-year-old married male who reported that he had had difficulty falling asleep for the previous four or five years. His sleep pattern prior to treatment was to try to fall asleep at about midnight but to be unable to sleep until three and sometimes four o'clock in the morning. Between midnight and four, the subject would worry about money, bills, his job, and so forth and finally turn on television to avoid worrying. Often he would fall asleep with the television still going.

The goal of the treatment was to bring sleeping under the stimulus control of the subject's bed and bedroom. To accomplish this he was given the following instructions:

1. Lie down intending to sleep only when you are sleepy.
2. Do not read or watch television in the bedroom.
3. If you find yourself unable to fall asleep,[1] get up and go into another room. Stay up as long as you wish and then return to the bedroom to sleep.
4. If you still cannot fall asleep, repeat step three. Do this as often as is necessary throughout the night.

No restrictions were made on the time and place for sexual activity. On such occasions, the instructions were to be followed afterward, when the subject intended to go to sleep. The above rules were to

---

[1] Although this instruction is vague, it was felt that any attempt to be more specific would have produced clock-watching and thus would exacerbate the problem of falling asleep.

form the basis for the development of permanent sleeping habits. Thus, the same rules were to be observed even after success was achieved.

The results as seen in Figure 2-3 are very clear. The treatment was successful in dramatically altering the subject's reported insomnia within two weeks. At the beginning of treatment, he had to get out of bed and leave the bedroom four or five times a night. At the end of two weeks, about half of the nights passed without his having to get up at all; and by the end of the follow-up period he had minor difficulty (getting up once during the night) less than once a week. The subject also reported that he was sleeping much better, getting from two to four hours more sleep per night than he had been getting before treatment. This marked improvement was confirmed by his wife.

Although a case study such as this is encouraging, it does not rule out coincidence or the subject's expectations for improvement as alternative explanations. Therefore, a comprehensive evaluation was executed (Bootzin, 1973). Seventy-eight severe insomniacs (recruited through newspaper advertisements in the Chicago area)

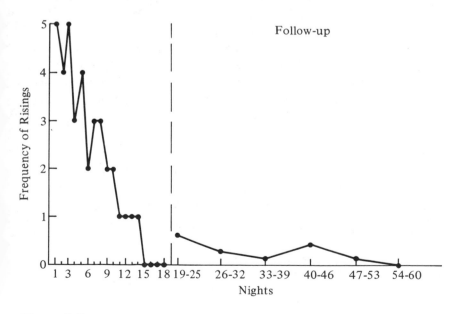

Figure 2-3
Frequency of nightly risings during treatment and follow-up. (From Bootzin, 1972.)

received one of four treatments: stimulus control instructions, relaxation training, relaxation scheduling, or no treatment. For the stimulus control subjects, two instructions were added to the four described above. They were:

5. Set your alarm and get up at the same time every morning irrespective of how much sleep you got during the night. This will help your body acquire a consistent sleep rhythm.
6. Do not nap during the day.

The relaxation training subjects were taught how to relax deeply and were instructed to practice twice a day. The relaxation scheduling subjects were also told to relax twice a day but did not receive any special training. The no treatment subjects were asked to keep extended records, after which they would receive treatment. The major measures of improvement were daily records kept by each subject for one month of the time it took to fall asleep, the number of hours slept, and the quality of sleep.

Before treatment, the insomniacs on the average took over 90 minutes a night to fall asleep and slept about 5.5 hours a night. From the baseline week to the last week of treatment, stimulus control subjects improved an average of 74 minutes in time to fall asleep as compared to improvement of 38, 15, and 24 minutes for relaxation training, relaxation scheduling, and no treatment subjects, respectively. Other results were that both stimulus control and relaxation training subjects averaged an hour more of sleep after treatment than subjects in the control groups; and at the end of treatment, stimulus control subjects rated themselves as feeling better upon awakening than subjects in the other groups.

In summary, stimulus control instructions were very effective in reducing insomnia across a number of measures. Relaxation training produced substantial improvement but did not match the degree of effectiveness produced by stimulus control.

Engaging in Incompatible Behavior

One way to decrease the frequency of a problem behavior is to engage in an incompatible behavior instead. This technique was an important part of the Stuart weight control programs described in the previous section. Thus, a person was instructed to engage in some high-probability behavior at the time he would find it most difficult to avoid eating. Since eating was not ordinarily associated with the behavior, there would be less of a disposition to eat while performing it. This technique probably more than any other is used by people trying to change some aspect of their behavior without professional help. Examples include sucking candy to reduce the urge to smoke, engaging in absorbing hobbies to "take my mind off worrying," and filing fingernails instead of biting them.

It is possible in the process of using this procedure to create a new problem while solving the old one—for example, using eating to control smoking although being overweight is just as undesirable. This may be a frequent occurrence because smoking is a habit for which there are few incompatible responses besides eating. Going for a walk cannot be used as a substitute since a person can take a package of cigarettes along. In fact, since smoking can be engaged in almost anywhere, at any time, only an activity that can be engaged in with the same high frequency across situations is likely to be a good substitute. It should not be surprising, then, that eating is often used to control smoking. Both may occur in a wide variety of situations, both require movements of the hand to the mouth, and both stimulate the inside of the mouth.

When overeating results from the attempt to control smoking, we could with some justification claim symptom substitution. But notice that our analysis indicated that it is not necessary to assume an underlying personality conflict. A new symptom resulted because of poor selection of an incompatible behavior. If the person had selected a response which was not a problem for him, it would not be called symptom substitution. Thus, sucking candy, chewing gum, or chewing on a pencil, if used as incompatible responses, would not be called symptoms even if used in all situations in which the person previously smoked. This analysis suggests the possibility that symptom substitution often occurs because of attempts to control a response with another conveniently available one that is also undesirable.

RELAXATION

Relaxation is probably one of the most frequently used incompatible behaviors engaged in to control anxiety and worry. There are other techniques, of course, such as physical exercise and hobbies, but in many situations relaxation is the preferred response. For example, relaxation training has been used successfully to reduce the stresses accompanying childbirth (e.g., Bing, 1967; Read, 1959).

Relaxation training has served as the basis of therapeutic endeavors as well. Edmund Jacobson (1938, 1964) in this country and Johannes Schultz and Wolfgang Luthe (1959) in Central Europe developed extensive therapies based entirely upon relaxation. Examples of problems for which relaxation is seen as an incompatible response include a variety of behavioral disorders such as insomnia, compulsions, phobias, and psychosomatic disorders.

Autogenic training. The Schultz and Luthe technique called autogenic training was developed after observing that people seemed to be able to induce physiological changes in themselves during hypnosis. The suggestion under hypnosis that an arm is getting heavy often elicits changes in muscle potential indicating that the person's arm is becoming very relaxed. Schultz speculated that a person could use language to elicit physiological changes without hypnosis. To accomplish this, a subject is told to suggest to himself that an arm is heavy. The subject practices this suggestion repeatedly, saying, "My arm is heavy, I am at peace, my arm is heavy"; each trial lasts from 30 to 60 seconds. According to Schultz and Luthe, it takes from three to six weeks for a subject to become accomplished at being able to relax any part of the body in this way. After a subject is able to make his whole body "heavy," similar procedures are followed for inducing warmth. Whereas the self-instruction of heaviness seems to elicit muscular relaxation, the self-instruction of warmth seems to elicit vasodilation. Following training in inducing warmth, the subject practices controlling heart rate, respiration, abdominal warmth, and cooling of the forehead. A number of case histories have been reported in which this training program successfully alleviated problem behavior.

In one report by Michael Kahn, Bruce Baker, and Jay Weiss (1968) the Schultz and Luthe procedure was evaluated as a solution for insomnia. Subjects received only the training dealing with heaviness and warmth. They were to practice a number of times each day and to use one long 5- to 10-minute trial before going to sleep. Even though the training period was short (two weeks),

11 of 13 subjects reported improvement in their ability to fall asleep. In addition, 7 of 8 who had reported that they were nervous, tense, or anxious before the study reported that they were less so afterward.

Progressive technique. In this country, the Jacobson technique for inducing relaxation, called progressive relaxation, has been used more frequently than the Schultz and Luthe technique. In fact, an abbreviated form of it is an essential component of a procedure called systematic desensitization which will be discussed in Chapter 4. Rather than relying upon self-suggestions of peace, heaviness, and warmth, Jacobson had subjects practice muscle relaxation directly by first discriminating tension and stress in various muscle groups, then by relaxing these groups. For example, an early instruction to a subject would be to bend the left hand as far back as possible and to notice the pattern of strain in the back of the hand and up the arm. After maintaining that position for one to two minutes the subject would be told to let the hand completely relax (Jacobson calls this "going negative") and to notice the difference in sensation at the points where previously strain had been felt. The object of the training program is to teach the subject what relaxation of each muscle group feels like and to provide practice at achieving more relaxation. A subject able to discriminate the patterns of tension in a muscle group is no longer told to tense before relaxing. Rather, he just relaxes the muscles from whatever level of tension they are at already.

The 12 relaxation lessons involving the eye region are reproduced here to illustrate the detail of the practice schedule:

Day	1	Wrinkle forehead
	2	Frown
	3	Relax only
	4	Close eyelids tightly
	5	Look left with lids closed
	6	Relax only
	7	Look right with lids closed
	8	Look up
	9	Relax only
	10	Look downward with lids closed
	11	Look forward with lids closed
	12	Relax only

Each lesson takes one hour. During it the subject tenses the specified muscles for three to four minutes and then relaxes them. This is repeated a few times until the subject is familiar with the sensation accompanying relaxation. The rest of the hour is spent "going negative" or relaxing only.

The training program proceeds slowly over a period of months. However, as subjects develop skill in relaxing, they are instructed to use relaxation as an incompatible response to control tension in a variety of everyday situations. Thus, a person who is tense while driving is instructed to apply the newly learned relaxation skill as much as possible while driving. This does not mean the driver closes his eyes while driving; rather, he tries to relax arm and leg muscles so that they are not tense. Obviously some tension is necessary for alert driving. However, it is not necessary to be so tense that the driver appears to be riveted to the wheel.

An interesting experiment comparing an accelerated progressive relaxation training program with other treatments was reported by Ray Zeisset (1968). Forty-eight male psychiatric inpatients at a Veterans Administration hospital were randomly assigned to one of four treatments designed to alleviate interview anxiety. Subjects were seen individually for four 50-minute sessions over a two-week period. One group of subjects received relaxation-plus-application training: during the first session, subjects received training in an accelerated form of Jacobson's procedure. They were also asked to practice the relaxation instructions between sessions for about 15 minutes twice a day. In the second session, they listened to a tape-recording of relaxation instructions followed by further practice of tension release cycles (tightening, holding, and releasing a muscle group). During the rest of the session, subjects practiced being relaxed while engaging in some simple activity such as turning an object with one hand. In the third session, subjects listened to an abbreviated relaxation tape in which no tensing of muscles was required. This was followed by more practice of relaxation while performing simple activities. In the fourth session, subjects relaxed without the tape and again participated in activities while remaining relaxed. The rest of this session was spent discussing the application of relaxation to everyday situations.

To control for the possibility that the attention of the therapist (and not relaxation training) caused improvement, another group of subjects received so-called attention treatment. These subjects did not receive relaxation training. Instead they were given the task of picking out an auditory signal from a background of noise. The rationale given to subjects was that this was a stressful task and that if the subjects built up tolerance for stress here, they would be better able to tolerate stress in other situations as well.

To control for the possibility of spontaneous improvement, a third group of subjects received no treatment and no contact. They participated only in the before and after treatment assessment procedures. The fourth group of subjects received systematic desensitization. Since this procedure has not been discussed in this chapter, the results for these subjects will not be presented in detail.

There were two assessment procedures: (1) the subjects' self-reports about how anxious they were in various situations, and (2) an objective behavioral measure. To provide the behavioral measure, subjects were seen individually for a five-minute interview during which their behavior was rated by two observers. The observers scored each patient for a number of anxiety indicators during the interview. Neither the observers nor the interviewer knew to which treatment subjects were assigned.

The results were that subjects receiving the relaxation-plus-application training both reported that they were less anxious and performed with less anxiety during the after-treatment interview than did subjects receiving either the attention control or the no-treatment control. (Subjects receiving the desensitization treatment performed as well as those receiving the relaxation-plus-application treatment.) This study indicates very clearly that even with abbreviated training, relaxation can be an important incompatible response for stress and anxiety. This experiment is particularly noteworthy in that the effectiveness of the relaxation training cannot be attributed to either coincidence or the attention of the therapist.

Since relaxation is so frequently advanced as a remedy for insomnia, a study comparing the effectiveness of progressive relaxation and autogenic training was performed (Nicassio and Bootzin, 1974). The methodology of the experiment was similar to that used in the evaluation of stimulus control instructions for insomnia described earlier. Thirty-seven insomniacs (recruited through newspaper advertisements) received one of four treatments: progressive relaxation, autogenic training, relaxation scheduling, or no treatment. Both progressive relaxation and autogenic training subjects were taught to relax using abbreviated forms of the respective techniques. Subjects were instructed to practice twice a day. The relaxation scheduling subjects were also told to relax twice a day but did not receive any special training. The no-treatment subjects were asked to keep extended records, after which they would receive treatment.

Both progressive relaxation and autogenic training resulted in decreases in time to fall asleep and higher global ratings of improvement, whereas relaxation scheduling and no treatment did not. Improvement was substantiated by reports from household members. Treatment gains in time to fall asleep were maintained at a six-month follow-up. Particularly important was the finding that the two techniques were markedly superior to relaxation scheduling. In order to produce improvement for severe insomniacs, it was not sufficient just to schedule time to relax; actual training in relaxation was required.

Although improvement was substantial, it should be remembered that relaxation training was still not as effective overall as was stimulus control (Bootzin, 1973). A combination of the two approaches (relaxation training and stimulus control instructions) may produce an even more effective treatment than either by itself.

Biofeedback. Another way to teach people to relax is by means of biofeedback training. Biofeedback is a method for providing immediate feedback about the ongoing functioning of one's own physiological systems. Typically this is done by presenting a visual or auditory stimulus which represents fluctuations in the biological system being monitored.

Electrical signals monitored from muscles (electromyogram, EMG) are related to the amount of tension in those muscles. Those electrical signals can be fed back to the subject by means of a tone or a light. For example, a tone could vary in pitch as the EMG varies in amplitude. Thus, a high tone could represent high levels of muscle tension while a low tone could represent low levels. Subjects can reduce muscle tension, then, by learning to keep the tone as low as possible for as long as possible. No one teaches subjects how to keep the tone low; they learn to do so through trial and error. In EMG feedback, shaping is also often employed. The feedback tone will be set initially to reflect rather high levels of muscle tension. As the subject becomes more accomplished, the sensitivity is changed so that less tension (more relaxation) is required to produce the same low tone.

Through biofeedback training, subjects can be taught to control biological responses such as blood pressure, heart rate, electroencephalogram (EEG) patterns, skin temperature, and stomach acid as well as EMG. There is considerable potential for clinical applications. Biofeedback training may provide the technology to help people learn to lower their blood pressure or to avoid ulcers by controlling their stomach acid, or to avoid heart problems by controlling cardiovascular responses. For the most part, however, biofeedback training is still in its experimental development stages. As yet, the clinical potential is unrealized. (See Blanchard and Young, 1974, for a review of the clinical application of biofeedback training.) An exception has been the use of biofeedback with tension headaches. Here, biofeedback has been remarkably effective.

Tension headaches are usually due to sustained contraction of the scalp and neck muscles. Thomas Budzynski, Johann Stoyva, Charles Adler, and Daniel Mullaney (1973) evaluated EMG biofeedback training for tension headaches. Their previous research had indicated that training subjects to reduce muscle tension in the forehead resulted in general relaxation including muscles in the scalp and neck. Therefore they used frontalis EMG feedback.

Eighteen subjects who complained of severe tension headaches were recruited. One-third of the subjects received feedback sessions twice a week (clicks were used as the feedback stimulus) and were instructed to practice relaxation at home twice daily. Another third of the subjects were given pseudofeedback sessions. In these sessions, subjects heard the EMG feedback recorded from other subjects. In other words, they never monitored their own levels of tension. During these sessions, subjects were told to listen to the clicks as a way of helping to suppress intruding thoughts. These subjects were also told to practice relaxation at home twice a day. The last third of the subjects merely kept records of their headache activity (as did the other subjects) for a two-month period before beginning their own feedback training.

The training resulted in much lower levels of muscle tension in the forehead for those subjects receiving actual feedback. In addition, only these subjects showed decreases in the number and intensity of headaches they had each day. Their dramatic improvement was maintained during a three-month follow-up. Control subjects were offered real feedback at the end of the study and they too improved.

This study is a clear demonstration that biofeedback can be an effective method for assisting subjects in learning to relax. Other studies demonstrating additional clinical applications of biofeedback training are sure to follow.

Summary

In this chapter, basic principles of behavior change were introduced using examples taken from attempts to change common, everyday problems. The following chapters will extend the discussion to more behavioral disorders and will discuss the complexities that arise in attempting to apply behavior change principles to such behavior.

3

Contingency Management

In this chapter we will explore in more detail the principles of changing behavior by controlling consequences. To apply these principles, it is essential that the consequences of a response can, in fact, be controlled—this seems almost too obvious to mention. After all, contingency management *is* the managing of contingencies. However, there are many situations in which contingencies are difficult to control because the cooperation of too many people in the subject's environment is required.

For this reason, much of the work extending contingency management principles has been done in institutional settings where it is easier to engineer the environment. Some investigators have explored contingency management in less restricted surroundings such as schools and homes. A look at the varied settings where contingency managers are found will provide a sample of the range of problems and the difficulties (theoretical and practical) still to be resolved.

The Mental Hospital

PSYCHOTIC CHILDREN

Contingency management within the mental hospital is often a last-ditch effort. Psychotic children, for instance, have shown remarkable resistance to conventional treatment. Their behavior is so impoverished, and they exhibit so many deficits, it is hard to know where to begin treatment.

These children engage mostly in self-stimulatory behavior—ranging from incessant rocking to self-destructive behavior such as head-banging. They are typically withdrawn and unresponsive to praise and other social reinforcement, and often mute (a few vowel sounds used during tantrums may be their entire repertoire). Those who can talk often use echolalic speech, which means they imitate words but do not use them to communicate.

Investigators have found speech is a good predictor of future adjustment for severely disturbed children. If some imitative speech is used before the age of five a child's chances of adjustment are improved, whereas without speech, a child tends to remain socially withdrawn and often spends his life in institutions.

O. Ivar Lovaas (1968) developed an intensive and comprehensive program designed to build appropriate behaviors in psychotic children. Because speech is so crucial, it was the focus of much of the program. First, children were taught to imitate sounds and words, and later they were taught meaning or the context for speech. The first children with whom Lovaas and his associates (Lovaas et al., 1966) worked had very limited vocal capabilities. Occasionally they used vowels (primarily during tantrums). These sounds were not similar to the babbling one would expect of pre-speech infants.

Speech training took place six days a week, seven hours a day, with a 15-minute break for every hour of training. The child and his adult trainer sat very close facing one another. Food was used as the reinforcer since previously social reinforcers had been used with no effect. Whenever a child gave the correct response he was given a single spoonful of food. Incorrect vocal responses were never punished.

There was punishment for nonverbal responses that interfered with the training. If a child threw a tantrum or engaged in self-destructive behavior, Lovaas and his associates used punishing stimuli (i.e., spanking and shouting). Within the first week, most punished behaviors including inattention were suppressed.

The first part of the Lovaas speech acquisition program had four steps. During step one the trainer rewarded all vocalization and would play with and fondle the child, and punishment was avoided. In addition, the child was rewarded for looking at the trainer's mouth. The goal was to develop imitation, and imitation requires observation. The trainer stayed at step one until the child was emitting one vocal response every five seconds and was fixating on the trainer's mouth 50 percent of the time.

During step two the trainer modeled a response (for example, said "baby") and reinforced the child for any sound at all made within six seconds. Step two continued until the child was responding three times more within the six-second interval than he had at the start of training.

Step three was the heart of the training program. During this step the child was rewarded only if the sound produced resembled the modeled sound. The first sounds taught in this step had three characteristics.

First, they could be *prompted*. This can be best explained by an example. For instance, to prompt the sound for the letter *b* the trainer held the child's lips together with the ends of his fingers and let go when the child exhaled. In other words, the child was physically aided in the attempt to produce the sound *b*. After a few trials, the prompt was *faded*. This means that the trainer gave the child less help each time—first by loosening the hold on the child's lips, then by moving his hand to the child's cheek, then the jaw, and then finally asking for the response without a prompt.

The second characteristic of early sounds was that they involved noticeable lip movement. These movements could be exaggerated for sounds such as "mm" or "ah." Sounds which require little visible movement are harder to learn; gutteral sounds, such as "k" and "g," are very difficult.

The third characteristic of these first sounds was that the child had already emitted them during step one and thus they were ones that the child could easily master. The criterion for mastery was set at 10 correct consecutive imitations.

After the child had mastered a sound, the trainer moved to step four by introducing a new sound. This sound was different from the ones learned in step three. During step four the step three procedures were used except that every once in a while the old sounds were interspersed to keep the child's discrimination sharp. This procedure then was recycled for more and more new sounds. Figure 3-1 presents the sounds and words that one child in the program, Billy, was able to master in the first 26 days of training. As can be seen from the figure, at first it took Billy several days

Figure 3-1

Acquisition of verbal imitation by Billy. Words and sounds are printed in lower-case letters on the days they were introduced and in capital letters on the days they were mastered. (From Lovaas et al., 1966.)

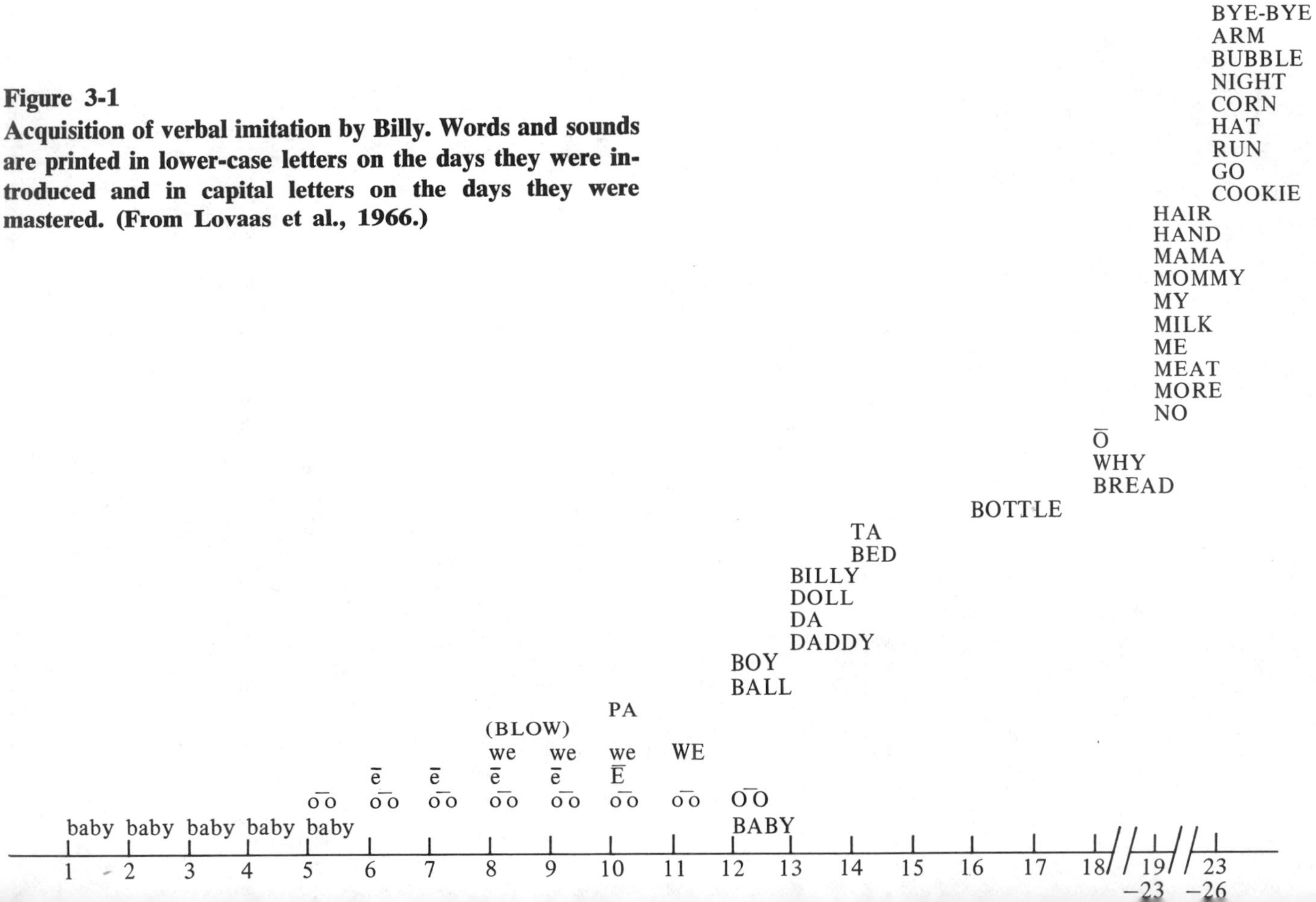

BYE-BYE
ARM
BUBBLE
NIGHT
CORN
HAT
RUN
GO
COOKIE

HAIR
HAND
MAMA
MOMMY
MY
MILK
ME
MEAT
MORE
NO

$\bar{O}$
WHY
BREAD

BOTTLE

TA
BED

BILLY
DOLL
DA
DADDY

BOY
BALL

$\overline{OO}$
BABY

WE

PA
we
$\bar{E}$
$\overline{oo}$

(BLOW)
we
$\bar{e}$
$\overline{oo}$

$\bar{e}$
$\overline{oo}$

$\bar{e}$
$\overline{oo}$

$\overline{oo}$

baby baby baby baby

1 2 3 4 5 6 7 8 9 10 11 12 13 14 15 16 17 18/ /19/ /23
−23 −26

to master a sound. Later he was able to master more than one word in a day.

Was reinforcement for correct responses responsible for these remarkable gains, or would the same gains have been achieved had the children received reinforcement irrespective of performance? To test this possibility, the children were given the usual number of reinforcements during one series of training trials, but this time they were noncontingent. This means that the child did not have to give the correct response to be reinforced. Rather, after a certain amount of training time had elapsed, the trainer reinforced the child no matter what the child's last response had been. Under noncontingent reinforcement, imitative behavior deteriorated rapidly. It seems obvious that contingent reinforcement (reinforcement given only after a correct response) was very important in maintaining the imitating behavior of these children.

After the children had acquired imitative speech, they were next taught the context for speech (meaning). Lovaas divided this part of the training into three steps. First, the children were taught to make verbal responses to nonverbal stimuli. Examples included attaching labels to objects (calling a chair a chair) and learning the proper use of pronouns and prepositions. Second, the children were taught to make nonverbal responses to verbal stimuli, for example, to follow instructions. These tasks were arranged so that the child first learned to follow simple instructions, then was taught to follow more elaborate ones. Third, the children were taught to give verbal responses to verbal stimuli. This varied from answering simple questions to carrying on a rather prolonged conversation.

Extraordinary patience was required of trainers, as it took as many as seven thousand trials just to teach the child to label accurately two different objects. However, as the children progressed through the program they were able to learn the new discriminations at a faster and faster rate. In addition to learning the words, they were learning how to learn. It should be emphasized that the children had not just learned a number of rote verbal responses. In fact, at the more complicated stages of training, children began to construct new sentences to express themselves. They had truly learned to use language.

Because of the intensive nature of the program, only three or four children participated at a time. The first two groups treated on an inpatient basis at the institute showed a decrease in inappropriate behaviors such as self-stimulation and echolalia and an increase in appropriate behaviors such as speech, play, and social nonverbal behavior. At the end of the 12- to 14-month treatment period, they were transferred to a local state hospital. A follow-up of these children three to four years later indicated their behavior had deteriorated considerably (Lovaas, Koegel, Simmons, and Long, 1973).

Because of this very discouraging follow-up, children who subsequently participated in the project were seen as outpatients throughout the treatment period. Parents were trained to continue the treatment program at home after the child was discharged. One- to two-year follow-up data are available for the first two groups treated as outpatients. These children maintained the gains made during treatment and in some areas continued to improve.

Technically, the maintenance of gains made during treatment is an example of stimulus generalization—i.e., it is a transfer of the treatment effects to other stimulus conditions or situations.

An important principle to be stressed throughout this chapter is that generalization should be planned, rather than depended upon as an inadvertent result of a treatment program. In this instance, treatment gains were maintained only when the environment to which the children would be released was programmed to continue the treatment. Despite the startling difference between the hospitalized children and those returned to their parents, the data should be interpreted with caution. Children were not randomly assigned to hospital or home, so it is possible that those children who maintained their improvement would have done so in any environment.

PSYCHOTIC ADULTS

Procedures similar to the Lovaas program for psychotic children have been used by Wayne Isaacs, James Thomas, and Israel Goldiamond (1960) with two adult *mute* schizophrenics. In this instance, the patients at one time had spoken fluently, so the treatment program was designed to provide incentives to reinstate speech. Even so, the therapists felt it necessary to gradually shape speech by reinforcing successive approximations.

The treatment program for one of the two patients will be described. He had been mute and hospitalized for 19 years. Cigarettes had been offered as a reinforcer without effect. One day a package of chewing gum accidently fell out of the therapist's pocket. The patient's eyes moved toward the gum and then returned to their usual straight-ahead position. This response was taken as evidence that chewing gum could be used as the reinforcer.

The therapist started meeting with the patient three times a week. During the first two weeks a stick of gum was held in front of the patient until his eyes moved toward it. When this response occurred, the therapist gave him the gum. By the end of the second week the patient moved his eyes toward the gum whenever it was presented. Notice how little was required of the patient. He was being reinforced for a behavior that he previously had exhibited. Giving the patient gum increased the frequency of the response that preceded it (looking at the gum), and confirmed the gum's reinforcing value.

Having confirmed the strength of the reinforcer, the therapist proceeded with the treatment. During the third week, the therapist waited for movement in the subject's lips before giving him the gum. By the end of this week both lip and eye movement occurred whenever the gum was held up. The therapist then withheld the gum until the patient made a sound. By the end of the fourth week the sight of the gum elicited eye movement, lip movement, and "a vocalization resembling a croak."

During the sessions in the fifth and sixth weeks, the therapist held up the gum and said, "Say gum, gum." Any vocalization was still reinforced. At the end of the sixth week, after the request the patient spontaneously said, "Gum, please." These were the first words anyone had heard from him in 19 years. Subsequently, he briefly answered questions. However, he responded only to the therapist and not to others.

Note that in the early steps the therapist did not wait for verbal behavior from the patient before reinforcing him. He reinforced successive approximations to verbal behavior. Such painstaking shaping is not always necessary, and we do not know that it was essential in this case. Perhaps if the therapist had requested and reinforced spoken words from the beginning of treatment, this, too, would have been effective. That seems unlikely because the patient would have had to make a very difficult transition all at once. In contrast, in the shaping procedure the responses required for reinforcement were such that he always had a high probability of being reinforced.

The problem still remained that only the therapist could elicit speech from the patient. In order to produce generalization to other people, a nurse joined the sessions. After a month, the patient would answer her questions also. After this achievement, workers on the ward were told not to respond to the patient's non-verbal requests. For example, previously, the patient had brought a volunteer his coat as a way of indicating that he wanted to go outside. Now the instruction required that the patient verbalize his requests. As a result, the patient started making verbal requests regularly.

Three things are particularly important about this study. One, the response was slowly shaped by means of successive approximations. Two, generalization was planned—first with the nurse, and then with other ward personnel. Three, the external, and somewhat artificial, reinforcer (gum) was replaced by naturally occurring reinforcers available on the ward (the compliance with requests).

This last point is especially noteworthy. Most behavior is not maintained by tangible extrinsic reinforcers, but by naturally occurring consequences in our social world. The use of chewing gum may have been necessary to initiate behavior change; however, it is equally important that the patient's speech eventually came under the control of the natural consequences in his environment. It would be very unlikely that he would maintain normal speech beyond treatment if this were not the case. Once again, for the *maintenance* of behavior change, the most important therapeutic agents are the people available in the subject's environment.

Multiple problem behavior. The work of Teodoro Ayllon has served as the impetus for much of the application of contingency management to behavior in mental hospitals. One investigation (Allyon, 1963) is particularly illuminating since it dealt with the intensive treatment of a patient who had a number of problems. This patient was a 47-year-old woman who had been hospitalized for nine years. She weighed 250 pounds (maintaining this weight by stealing food from other patients in the dining room); she hoarded towels in her room; and she wore about 25 pounds of excess clothing (a half-dozen dresses at a time, several sweaters, etc.). In order to treat her problems, Ayllon set up a separate program for each of them.

The first program dealt with her stealing of food. Previously, the hospital physicians had prescribed a diet to help the patient lose her unhealthy excessive weight and the ward staff had tried persuasion to keep her on her diet—to no avail. Then the staff tried forcing her to return the stolen food. This also was ineffective—and time consuming.

It is easy to understand why these procedures had been no help in suppressing stealing. The punishment was mild and it occurred late in the chain of responses involved in stealing. Because the punishment occurred after the food had been taken, it is likely that occasionally the patient was able to eat some of the food before she was caught. Thus, stealing was being reinforced intermittently. If a response is reinforced intermittently, it is generally more difficult to extinguish. Thus, the overall effect of the staff's procedures was to make stealing food more resistant to extinction.

Ayllon's behavior modification treatment specified that the patient was to be removed from the dining room if she approached a table other than her own or if she picked up unauthorized food from the dining room counter. In other words, if the patient engaged in behavior that led to stealing food, she faced the consequence of terminating the meal early. No instructions were given to the patient; the new consequences were automatically instituted.

Figure 3-2 shows the amount of stealing after the consequences were altered. As can be seen by the graph, food stealing dropped to almost zero immediately with just a couple of reoccurrences. Since the patient was now sticking to her diet, she started to lose weight. A year after the contingencies to control stealing were changed, she weighed in at about 180 pounds, a loss of 70 pounds.

The patient's second problem behavior was towel hoarding. Throughout her hospitalization, the patient collected towels in her room. The ward staff continuously had to retrieve their towels, but she still was able to keep between 19 and 29 towels in her room at any one time.

Ayllon instructed the ward staff to give her towels instead of taking them away. The first week she was given about seven towels a day. No attempt was made to retrieve them, and the staff was instructed not to react with disapproval to any attempts by the patient to gather additional towels. This treatment is analogous to *stimulus satiation* (a stimulus is less reinforcing if it is continuously available). However, more was involved than just satiation. There

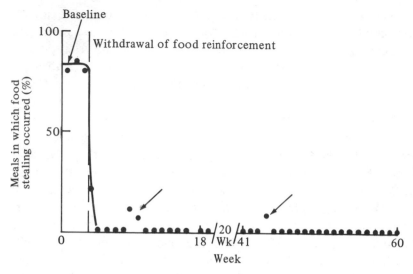

Figure 3-2
A response, food stealing, is eliminated when it results in the withdrawal of food reinforcement. The arrows indicate the rare occasions when food stealing occurred. For purposes of presentation,
a segment comprising 20 weeks during which no stealing occurred
is not included. (From Ayllon, 1963.)

was also the dramatic shift in the consequences for collecting
towels.

At first the patient enjoyed the change enormously. She would
thank the nursing staff for each towel they gave her and she would
walk around holding a towel next to her cheek. However, when the
number of towels in her room reached 625, she started removing
some of them. At that point, no more towels were given to her.
Figure 3-3 presents the results.

Her comments as the experiment proceeded are of interest:

> *First week:* As the nurse entered the patient's room carrying a
> towel, the patient would smile and say, "Oh, you found it for me,
> thank you." *Second week:* When the number of towels given to the
> patient increased rapidly, she told the nurses, "Don't give me no
> more towels. I've got enough towels. I've got enough." *Third week:*
> "Take them towels away. . . . I can't sit here all night and fold
> towels." *Fourth and fifth weeks:* "Get these dirty towels out of
> here." *Sixth week:* After she had started taking the towels out of
> her room, she remarked to the nurse, "I can't drag any more of
> these towels, I just can't do it" (Ayllon, 1963).

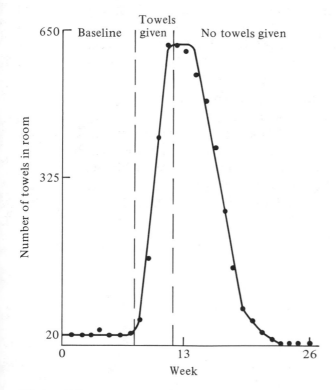

Figure 3-3
A response, towel hoarding, is eliminated when the patient is given towels in excess. When the number of towels reaches 625 the patient starts to discard them. She continues to do so until the number in her room averages 1.5 compared to the previous 20 towels per week. (From Ayllon, 1963.)

During a follow-up of over a year, the patient not once was observed hoarding towels.

The third problem, excess clothing, was perhaps the one that most prevented her from being released from the hospital. Ayllon's treatment was to set a weight limit which she had to meet to get into the dining room. The first limit was set at 23 pounds over her body weight. Thus, in order to eat, she had to discard 2 pounds of clothing. Sometimes, the patient discarded more clothing than was necessary. Each time that occurred, the weight limit was adjusted down so she would have to continue wearing fewer clothes. Figure 3-4 shows the results of this experiment. At the end of the experiment, the patient was wearing 3 pounds of clothing, a drop of 22 pounds.

An interesting sidelight is that after the experiment the patient's parents visited and asked to take her home for a visit for the first time in nine years. Previously, they had not been interested since they considered her appearance embarrassing.

This patient's problem behaviors, although easily modified, are serious. Stealing food, hoarding towels, and wearing 25 pounds of clothing at one time are the type of behaviors which prolong hospitalization. There are not many people (including relatives, landlords, and residents of boarding houses) who would tolerate living with a person exhibiting these behaviors. It was only after

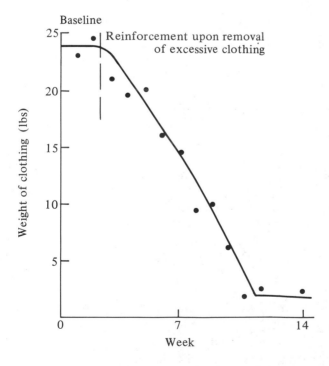

Figure 3-4
A response, excessive dressing, is eliminated when food reinforcement is made dependent upon removal of superfluous clothing. Once the weight of the clothing worn by the patient drops to three pounds it remains stable. (From Ayllon, 1963.)

improvement in these behaviors that the interest of the patient's relatives was rekindled.

The Token Economy

The preceding examples of the use of reinforcement in the mental hospital indicate that contingency management has considerable potential for altering behavior in such settings. Encouraged by these results, some investigators have attempted to engineer the entire ward environment so that appropriate behavior will be reinforced and inappropriate behavior extinguished. Such programs are called *token economies,* since appropriate behavior is reinforced with tangible conditioned reinforcers (tokens) rather than with the back-up reinforcers themselves. Conditioned reinforcers have a number of advantages, as you recall from the discussion in Chapter 2.

First, tokens can be dispensed for increments of improvement in instances in which the back-up reinforcer could not. In a mental hospital it is often effective to use home visits as a reinforcer. Visits would be impractical to dispense for small improvements, but tokens, which could be accumulated and later exchanged for a visit home, are feasible.

Second, tokens provide a visible record of improvement. This may facilitate social reinforcement from staff members as well as self-reinforcement. In addition, it becomes easier to spot patients who are not improving and to alter the treatment program accordingly.

Third, the timing of reinforcement is more easily controlled with tokens. It is often the case that more improvement is made if reinforcement immediately follows an appropriate response. This can be accomplished conveniently by having staff members carry tokens to reinforce appropriate behavior as it occurs. Carrying tokens also reminds staff members to look for behavior to reinforce.

Fourth, if tokens are exchangeable for a variety of back-up reinforcers (such as food, cigarettes, television, visits home), the tokens do not lose their value if the patient becomes satiated on some back-up reinforcers. Thus, if food were the only reinforcer, its effectiveness would vary depending on whether the subject was deprived or satiated.

Fifth, tokens provide a convenient way of dealing with individual differences. What is reinforcing for one person is not necessarily reinforcing for someone else. However, it would be impractical to develop a comprehensive program in which some patients were being reinforced directly with food, others with time off the ward, and so forth. The staff would have to remember who was being reinforced with what, and all reinforcers would have to be available all of the time. In a token economy, tokens are used to reinforce all patients and each patient can exchange tokens for whatever reinforcer he or she wants.

Which behaviors are reinforced? The first step in starting a token economy is deciding what behaviors should be reinforced. To assess their deficits, patients must be observed and their behavior recorded in detail. The first token economies were established on custodial back wards where long-term patients who exhibited many behavioral deficits were confined. The behavior of patients on such wards could be best labelled as apathetic. During the day they either slept (on the floor if allowed) or sat staring blankly. When they walked, their movements tended to be rather slow. Even self-care behaviors deteriorated markedly. Male patients were unshaven and looked as if they had been wearing the same clothes for weeks; female patients did not comb their hair and also looked disheveled. They engaged in very little self-initiated behavior. What little activity occurred was at the request and direction of staff members.

What, then, are appropriate goals for such a patient population? Obviously the first steps must increase activity level and improve self-care behaviors. Only after these very basic steps are accomplished is it possible to plan for the return of these patients to the community. Thus, most token programs for long-term hospitalized patients reinforce self-care behaviors. Workskills are reinforced, not just to increase activity level but because they are activities which are relevant to the patient's adjustment after leaving the hospital. The person who is able to work has more options available. Even elementary activities such as dusting, washing, and other housekeeping activities are skills which would be valued and reinforced in a number of posthospital settings.

Since many patients are rather withdrawn, social interaction is often reinforced. Some programs have not reinforced these behaviors directly but have noted whether changes in them occur. Technically this would be called response generalization. Whereas stimulus generalization is the spread of treatment effects to new situations, response generalization is the spread of these effects to responses that were not specifically reinforced.

Which reinforcers are used? As mentioned earlier, tokens are likely to be more effective and more valued if there is a large variety of back-up reinforcers. Usually the Premack Principle is used to identify potential reinforcers, which are then made exchangeable for tokens. In some programs, tokens may be exchanged for cigarettes; in others, cigarettes are provided but tokens are required to enter the dining room. The variety of activities for which tokens may be exchanged include television, canteen privileges, leaving the ward, having a private room, and passes off the grounds.

Table 3-1 lists the back-up reinforcers used in the first comprehensive token economy in a mental hospital. It was developed by Teodoro Ayllon and Nathan Azrin (1965) for female hospitalized mental patients whose average age was 47 and who had spent an average of nine years in the hospital.

Since many patients on chronic wards engage in few activities, it seems paradoxical to charge tokens for some things which might appropriately be goals instead of privileges. For example, some patients are very reluctant to leave the ward. To deal with the problem of reluctance to use reinforcers, Ayllon and Azrin (1968) recommended reinforcement sampling and exposure. Each patient would be allowed to sample each reinforcement before being charged tokens for it. If this was not sufficient, the patient also would be exposed to the reinforcement in such a way as to maximize participation (e.g., by seeing others using it).

Other investigators have dealt with this difficulty by using individual contracts with patients. Patients who were reluctant to go on passes could earn tokens for doing so. Other patients who preferred passes would be charged tokens. A system with many individual contracts is harder to administer, but it has the advantage of focusing more directly on each patient's difficulties.

Problems in administering a token economy. There are a number of practical difficulties in administering a comprehensive token program. Perhaps the major problem is ensuring that the reinforcers remain effective. This requires that they not be available outside of the program. To accomplish this a number of decisions have to be made regarding gifts from relatives, borrowing and lending, stealing, selling, and gambling.

Table 3-1
Reinforcers Available for Tokens

REINFORCER	No. OF TOKENS DAILY
I. Privacy	
Selection of room 1	0
Selection of room 2	4
Selection of room 3	8
Selection of room 4	15
Selection of room 5	30
Personal chair	1
Choice of eating group	1
Screen (room divider)	1
Choice of bedspreads	1
Coat rack	1
Personal cabinet	2
Placebo	1–2
II. Leave from the ward	
20-min walk on hospital grounds (with escort)	2
30-min grounds pass (3 tokens for each additional 30 min)	10
Trip to town (with escort)	100
III. Social interaction with staff	
Private audience with chaplain, nurse	5 min free
Private audience with ward staff, ward physician (for additional time—1 token per min)	5 min free
Private audience with ward psychologist	20
Private audience with social worker	100
IV. Devotional opportunities	
Extra religious services on ward	1
Extra religious services off ward	10
V. Recreational opportunities	
Movie on ward	1
Opportunity to listen to a live band	1
Exclusive use of a radio	1
Television (choice of program)	3

REINFORCER	No. of TOKENS DAILY
VI. Commissary items	
Consumable items such as candy, milk, cigarettes, coffee, and sandwich	1–5
Toilet articles such as Kleenex, toothpaste, comb, lipstick, and talcum powder	1–10
Clothing and accessories such as gloves, headscarf, house slippers, handbag, and skirt	12–400
Reading and writing materials such as stationery, pen, greeting card, newspaper, and magazine	2–5
Miscellaneous items such as ashtray, throw rug, potted plant, picture holder, and stuffed animal	1–50

From Ayllon and Azrin, 1965. Additional experiments are found in Ayllon and Azrin, 1968.

Some of these activities (e.g., borrowing, selling, and gambling) involve rudimentary social interaction that could justifiably be encouraged. However, if allowed to flourish they undermine the effectiveness of the token program, so they are usually prohibited. Such behaviors can be controlled by a system of fines. Thus, they are treated much as any other reinforcing activity. Residents may borrow, sell, or gamble, but it costs tokens to do so.

To prevent unauthorized exchanges of tokens, some programs individualize the tokens by printing each patient's initials on them—they are then useless to anyone else. A more frequent solution is to individualize the tokens of the few patients who seem to be out of the program. For example, patients who give away (or steal) tokens could be given different colored ones than the rest of the patients.

If patients are giving away tokens it indicates the tokens have not acquired any value for them. Such patients may require a prolonged period of training in which the tokens are used as discriminative stimuli for the back-up reinforcers. Thus, when a patient wants a cigarette he could be given a token which would be immediately exchanged for one. This would be repeated until the patient was well practiced at handing tokens to ward personnel for back-up reinforcers. Then delay could be developed systematically. At first the patient might be required to keep the token for only 30 seconds before exchanging it; then one minute; and so on.

The effectiveness of token economies. There is no doubt token economies have been successful in altering those behaviors upon which they have focused. This has been true whether the target responses have been self-care behaviors, work activities, social interaction, aggressiveness, or symptomatic behavior (see Kazdin and Bootzin, 1972, for a review of the effectiveness of token economies). In addition, many investigators have reported generalized effects. For example, John Atthowe and Leonard Krasner (1968) reported that after the initiation of a token economy at a Veterans Administration hospital the discharge rate increased. The authors attribute the discharges to a general lessening of apathy—in fact, they described their ward as "jumping."

Generalization. Although there have been numerous demonstrations of the effectiveness of token reinforcement in changing behavior, there has been remarkably little research on whether behaviors modified in the hospital generalize to the outside community. If anything, most research indicates behavior deteriorates rapidly if not maintained by reinforcement in the new setting.

The only evidence that generalization occurs across situations is that some programs report increased discharged rates along with decreased readmission rates. However, these measures are rather imprecise, and results based on them may be due to a number of factors besides the effectiveness of the token program. Since discharge and readmission rates depend upon administrative decisions, increases and decreases can be accomplished without concomitant changes in the patient's psychological status. It is possible that a staff dedicated to a high discharge rate will work much harder to find appropriate patient placement in the community and will complete the paper work necessary to make a high discharge rate possible. Another staff, one that is more interested in changing behavior within the hospital, may dramatically alter the behavior of its patients on the ward and yet have a low discharge rate.

Similar considerations may affect readmission rates. Staffs dedicated to keeping people in the community could make it difficult for patients to reapply and be readmitted. Such a staff might prefer to offer outpatient treatment and assistance in dealing with an immediate crisis. Other admitting staffs may take just the opposite orientation and admit every patient who applies.

In the past few years, community psychology and psychiatry programs have swept the country. The implication for discharge and readmission has been clear. Hospital staffs have been encouraged to discharge patients and develop community resources so that patients can be treated without requiring prolonged hospitalization. Any administrator who contrasts discharge and readmission rates before and after the introduction of a new program is likely to find statistics to support the program. Thus, it is not clear whether token economies are more successful at keeping people in the community or have benefited from a change in the orientation of hospital staffs. Whichever the case, as stated before, generalization should be planned, rather than depended upon as an inadvertent result of the program.

Generalization techniques. A variety of techniques have been used to increase generalization (Kazdin and Bootzin, 1972). The most frequently used procedure is to follow a rule proposed by Ayllon and Azrin: "Teach only those behaviors that will continue to be reinforced after training." Behaviors should be selected that will come under the control of naturally occuring reinforcers in the person's environment.

A second procedure to increase generalization is to fade token reinforcement gradually, substituting social approval, extra privileges, and other naturally occurring consequences. Fading sometimes has been systematized into a step program in which patients begin at an intitial level and, depending upon improvement and sustained performance, progress to higher levels. At each higher level, the patient receives added privileges but must meet more stringent criteria for reinforcement. It is hoped that the patients will maintain their gains when released since they already will have had considerable experience in performing appropriately without token reinforcement. Although step systems have considerable intuitive appeal, there have not yet been unambiguous follow-up data justifying their use. Additional studies investigating programmed generalization are badly needed.

Token economies have achieved remarkable changes in patient behavior; however, they are probably not the entire answer to the mental health problem. Although they focus on relevant behaviors (that is, developing behaviors that are likely to be adaptive in the community), they do this in a very artificial setting (the mental hospital). A more fruitful approach calls not only for the development of relevant behaviors, but also for the development of those behaviors in the actual settings in which they will be practiced.

George Fairweather and his associates (Fairweather et al., 1969) have led the way by suggesting self-help lodges as an alternative to the mental hospital. Most patients do not need the constant surveillance and medical facilities of the mental hospital. In addition, there is as wide a variety of skills found in a community of patients as would be found in any collection of people gathered at random. Therefore, self-supporting patient communities would be possible.

In Fairweather's program, patients were trained in the hospital for roles that would be required in the lodge. The plan was to transfer a group of patients to the lodge and provide them with less and less assistance over time. A major problem was that very little that was learned in the hospital actually transferred to the lodge. For example, after intensive in-hospital training on grocery shopping, the cook spent the entire first week's food budget on beer and ice cream. The long training period was mostly ineffective; the skills had to be learned in the lodge itself. Once skills were learned, the program became a therapeutic success. Patients living in the lodge eventually were completely independent of the hospital and were able to maintain themselves successfully in the community.

The problems in transferring the program from the hospital to the community are ones which are surely encountered by other programs as well. The most efficient and effective programs are likely to be those that alter the consequences of the behavior in the environment in which it is a problem.

Token economies and the law. Beginning in the late 1960s, many aspects of prison life were subjected to judicial review after complaints that prisoners were being deprived of their constitutional rights. Some of the legal concepts developed in the prisoners' rights movement have recently been applied to institutionalized mental patients as well. Although no court decisions have been concerned directly with token economies in mental hospitals, a number of inferences can be drawn from the direction of the decisions that have been rendered.

Since 1966, the courts have interpreted the Thirteenth Amendment's prohibition against involuntary servitude as a prohibition against forced patient labor which has no purpose other than to save the institution money. In a decision applying to Alabama institutions (*Wyatt v. Stickney*, 1972), this principle was expanded to prohibit all involuntary patient labor, whether therapeutic or not, which involves institutional operation or maintenance. Voluntary labor was permitted under the *Wyatt* standard if patients received compensation according to the federal minimum wage law.

There is little doubt that many institutions have abused patient labor. But it is also true that work skills are often the most appropriate response to be developed if return to the community is a primary goal, and a number of token economies have used work behaviors as target responses.

As David Wexler (1973) has pointed out, many forms of institutional labor, although cost-saving, prevent apathy and prepare patients for life outside the hospital. The implication of the *Wyatt* standard is that entire categories of work opportunities would not be available unless patients were paid the minimum wage. Only work unrelated to institutional operation would still be available, and much of this would of necessity be make-work. Work that is essential to the operation of an institution is often more rewarding than make-work because the patient can see what is being accomplished, and thus this work is likely to be more therapeutic. A likely consequence of the minimum wage requirement is that administrators would hire permanent employees to do work that could have been of therapeutic benefit to patients.

It is true that safeguards are required to protect patients from institutional peonage, but these safeguards should not be so restrictive as to discourage the institution from discharging its obligation to provide treatment.

Even more important for the operation of token economies, the courts have begun to enumerate the rights guaranteed to institutionalized patients. In *Wyatt v. Stickney*, the court listed as absolute rights a number of items which frequently have been dispensed contingently in token economies. For example, *Wyatt* guarantees patients a comfortable bed and nutritionally adequate meals, as well as the right to have visitors, to use personal possessions, to attend religious services, to be outdoors regularly, and to have access to day rooms furnished with reading lamps, tables, chairs, television, and other recreational facilities.

Under such guidelines, token economies could still be used, but absolute rights could not be dispensed contingently. This would probably mean a greater reliance on individualized reinforcers. Reinforcer sampling might be used to help develop the effectiveness of new reinforcers. Unusual reinforcers such as special and not readily available foods and the opportunity to engage in unique activities have sometimes been used successfully in the past, and most token programs could be modified to rely more heavily upon them. However, the acquisition of many new reinforcers would mean additional expenditures.

This is a small price to pay in order to guarantee basic rights. Nevertheless, chronic psychotics sometimes do not respond except to the most basic reinforcers. Here there is a direct conflict between the right to treatment and the right to enjoy basic privileges. By depriving some patients of an effective treatment, we may be condemning them to a lifetime of institutionalization. Although general guidelines for the use of reinforcers certainly should be developed, and although it is possible for most programs with most patients to work within the *Wyatt* standard, probably it is wiser to allow some flexibility so all patients can have access to effective treatment.

The Classroom

Although much of the effort in using learning principles in the classroom has been applied toward curriculum reform (for example, programmed learning), here we will focus primarily on behavior problems in the classroom. This is not to say that curriculum and behavior problems are not related. An exciting and challenging curriculum is likely to decrease the frequency of disruptive behavior in the classroom. However, even the best curriculum is insufficient if the students have not acquired necessary work skills.

TOKEN REINFORCEMENT

One of the first systematic uses of contingency management to maintain academic behavior was done in an experimental situation. Arthur Staats and his colleagues (Staats et al., 1964) were attempting to investigate reading acquisition in four-year-old children. A method to keep the children motivated throughout the 20-minute sessions was required. To do this, Staats and his associates used a token reinforcement system. Each time a child made a correct response in a programmed learning device, a marble (the token) dropped from a dispenser in front of the child. The marble could then be immediately exchanged for a plastic trinket, a small piece of candy, or a penny. The child also had the alternative of saving the marbles for a more expensive toy by dropping the marble in a container beneath the toy that was desired. When the container was completely filled with marbles, the toy was the child's.

The children could save toward four different toys costing 10, 35, 80, and 150 marbles, respectively. To maximize the attractiveness of the toys, each child selected the toys to be placed above the containers from a larger selection. Figure 3-5 shows the arrangement of the experimental apparatus and toys. Providing the children with the opportunity to save toward more expensive toys was an effective means of avoiding satiation on candy and trinkets. Thus, the token reinforcement system was a successful way to maintain performance during the daily 20-minute sessions.

Comprehensive token economies within the classroom have been used as a way to improve academic performance in children having perceptual and motor handicaps, retarded children, and inner-city children showing severe learning deficits. Particularly impressive have been the programs with retarded children. In many settings retarded children are highly distractible. Yet with token reinforcement, it has been possible to increase their concentration. The procedure in most programs is to give tokens throughout the day for appropriate behavior. Then at the end of the day, the tokens can be exchanged in a classroom store for a variety of back-up reinforcers (including candy, toys, and clothes). A banking system is usually instituted so that children may save their tokens to apply toward expensive items.

What about generalization? The issue is slightly different in school classrooms than it is in psychiatric hospitals. For hospital programs, the question is whether the effects of token reinforcement given in the hospital will generalize to the community after the patient has been discharged; in classroom programs the issue is whether the effects will generalize to other classrooms, ones that the student either is in concurrently or will be in later.

There is considerable evidence that unless generalization is programmed, token economies in all settings produce behavior change only while contingent token reinforcement is being delivered. For example, reinforcement programs in classrooms which were implemented for only part of the day generally have not found evidence of generalization to the part of the day in which tokens were not dispensed (see Kazdin and Bootzin, 1972, for a review of this literature). Because of this limitation, it is better to use token economies only when there are very severe deficits to overcome.

Figure 3-5
The laboratory apparatus for the experimental study of reading behavior. The child is seated before the center panel. Letter stimuli appear in the small plexiglass windows in front of the child whenever he activates the pushbutton on the table before him. If a correct reading response sequence then occurs, the marble dispenser located at the child's near right drops a marble into a tray positioned at its base. To the child's left is an open bin into which are delivered trinkets, edibles, or pennies whenever the child deposits a marble in the funnel located atop the marble dispenser. A marble may also be "spent" on one of the toys displayed at the child's far right. (Redrawn from Staats et al., 1964.)

Then, as the student acquires the appropriate skills, token reinforcement can be faded and replaced with social approval and naturally occurring consequences.

DEALING WITH DISRUPTIVE BEHAVIOR

In most elementary school classrooms, children have already developed their work skills to a point at which tangible reinforcers are unnecessary. Nevertheless, disruptive behavior occurs occasionally in every classroom. To deal with it, teachers traditionally have relied upon punishment (particularly verbal disapproval). This has a number of unfortunate consequences. First, it is coercive and usually unpleasant. There is danger that learning activities will become aversive through their repeated association with unpleasant events.

Second, the teacher is providing a model of coercive control which the children may emulate. Most of us probably would prefer that our children learn to persuade rather than coerce others. Third, commands yelled by the teacher (e.g., "Johnny, sit down!") add to the noise level of the classroom and may thereby increase the children's distractibility. Fourth, some children are reinforced by teacher disapproval. They may be playing the role of class clown—sacrificing the teacher's approval for the approval of other children. Alternatively, teacher disapproval may be the only attention given to them by the teacher, and if the teacher's attention is valued, disapproval will be reinforcing. Fifth, verbal commands and disapproval are usually ineffective ways to suppress disruptive behavior. They are used so frequently, however, because they give the illusion of effectiveness.

An illustration of this last point was reported by Charles Madsen, Wesley Becker, and their colleagues (Madsen et al., 1968). They monitored out-of-seat behavior as a function of the teacher's sit-down commands, and found that when teachers increased the frequency of sit-down commands, the children more frequently got out of their seats. The child who was commanded to sit down obeyed for the moment, but other children were more likely to get up. Far from suppressing the frequency of out-of-seat behavior, teachers using sit-down commands were actually increasing it.

Praising appropriate behavior. If verbal commands and disapproval are not good ways to control disruptive behavior, what should the teacher do? Teachers can effectively minimize problem behavior by praising appropriate behavior rather than disapproving of inappropriate behavior. That the contingent use of praise can be dramatically effective in altering deviant behavior in the classroom has been adequately demonstrated. In one study (Becker et al., 1967) the average deviant behavior of problem children in five different classrooms decreased over 50 percent. To achieve these results teachers were given general rules to follow for the entire class and special supplementary rules for individual problem children. For example, here are the general rules and the set of special rules for one child, Alice (from Becker et al., 1967):

GENERAL RULES

1. Make explicit rules as to what is expected of children for each period. (Remind of rules when needed.)

2. Ignore (do not attend to) behaviors which interfere with learning or teaching, unless a child is being hurt by another. Use punishment which seems appropriate, preferably withdrawal of some positive reinforcement.
3. Give praise and attention to behaviors which facilitate learning. Tell child what he is being praised for. Try to reinforce behaviors incompatible with those you wish to decrease.
   Examples of how to praise: "I like the way you're working quietly." "That's the way I like to see you work." "Good job, you are doing fine."
   Transition period. "I see Johnny is ready to work." "I'm calling on you because you raised your hand." "I wish everyone were working as nicely as X," etc. Use variety and expression.

SPECIAL RULES FOR ALICE

Attempt to follow the general rules above, but try to give extra attention to Alice for the behavior noted below, but try not to overdo it to the extent that she is singled out by other children. Spread your attention around.
1. Praise sitting straight in chair with both feet and chair legs on floor and concentrating on own work.
2. Praise using hands for things other than sucking.
3. Praise attention to direction given by teacher or talks made by students.
4. Specify behavior you expect from her at beginning of day and new activity, such as sitting in chair facing front with feet on floor, attention to teacher and class members where appropriate, what she may do after assigned work is finished, raising hand to answer questions or get your attention.

Alice was eight years old. Her teacher considered her a "sulking child" since she would sometimes withdraw and not talk to anyone. In addition, she frequently sat inappropriately in her chair, sucked her thumb, and made frequent movements of her arms and legs. The instructions to her teacher, as you can see, emphasized praising appropriate behavior which would be incompatible with Alice's problem behavior. The inappropriate behavior was to be ignored.

Ignoring inappropriate behavior was the most difficult instruction for all teachers. The teachers were astonished to find how much of their own behavior was under the stimulus control of the children's misbehavior. Since many teachers felt compelled to do something when a child misbehaved, they were instructed to reinforce another child for some appropriate behavior. For example, rather than commanding Johnny to sit down when he was out of his seat, the teacher was instructed to find someone close to Johnny (e.g., Billy) who was working and say, "Billy, I like the way you are sitting at your desk and working." This is an effective way to apply the principle of *vicarious reinforcement*. Vicarious reinforcement refers to the reinforcing effects on an observer of witnessing reinforcement being delivered to someone else. In other words, Johnny is being vicariously reinforced for appropriate behavior because he witnesses Billy being directly reinforced. There is considerable laboratory evidence that vicarious reinforcement is an effective way to modify behavior. It appears to be equally effective in the classroom.

A teacher cannot ignore disruptive behavior when there is danger that someone will be hurt. In this case, is it more effective to reprimand publicly the misbehaving child, to reinforce publicly appropriate behavior in another child (vicarious reinforcement), or to intercede privately (i.e., go over to the child and quietly take him to his seat)? K. Daniel O'Leary and Wesley Becker (1968) studied such situations and found that vicarious reinforcement and private reprimands were equally effective while public reprimands were ineffective in decreasing the frequency of deviant behavior. Thus, the teacher who must intercede to prevent someone from being hurt should do so privately. Private reprimands are less likely to bring the inappropriate behavior to the attention of other children than are public reprimands.

Contingency contracting. Besides praise and disapproval, the teacher has a number of naturally occurring contingencies available which could be used to reinforce appropriate behavior. Classroom events which children enjoy can be used to reinforce on-task behavior. Lloyd Homme (1969) has suggested calling this procedure contingency contracting. In other words, the teacher and the children make a contract that class time will be arranged so that a certain amount of work will be followed by some activity or event that the children would enjoy. For example, if children prefer screaming and yelling to learning how to read, the teacher can reinforce one minute of reading with one minute of screaming and yelling. Using this method, the teacher can increase the time spent working without jeopardizing the enjoyment associated with it.

Although children's behavior changes when behavior modification procedures are instituted, so does the behavior of the teacher. In many ways it is a reciprocal relationship. The teacher is providing more of what the students want so that the students will give more of what the teacher wants. This suggests the possibility that students could be the ones taught behavior modification techniques, rather than teachers. It need not be a technology available only to those in authority.

TEACHING STUDENTS TO BE BEHAVIOR MODIFIERS

A fascinating account of a project in which students were taught behavior modification techniques has been reported by Paul Graubard and Harry Rosenberg (1974). They taught special education junior high school students to be what they called behavior engineers. Graubard and Rosenberg were consultants to the students rather than to the teachers.

Seven students from the special education class were instructed. All seven had been labeled by school officials and the police department as incorrigible. They met with their behavior modification consultants for one 40-minute period a day.

The students decided to try to encourage more positive behavior from their teachers. To do this they were taught to reinforce teachers by establishing eye contact, asking for extra help, sitting straight, nodding in agreement when the teacher spoke, and using reinforcing comments. They were also taught to break eye contact when being scolded, and to ignore provocations. The techniques were practiced repeatedly using role playing and videotapes.

After the students became adept at the techniques, they were reintegrated into their normal classes where they applied the procedures and kept track of their success. The students were successful in changing all of their teachers. Positive contacts increased and negative contacts decreased, and some students were able to extinguish negative contacts with teachers entirely. This is remarkable, since for some this was the only type of contact they had with teachers before the program began.

Near the end of the project, the students put their teachers on extinction and stopped all positive reinforcement. Positive responses from the teachers fell sharply but increased again when the students reinstituted reinforcement. As a result of the program, all students felt that they had more control of their lives and felt more positive about themselves.

THE COLLEGE CLASSROOM

Not all work with contingency management in educational settings has taken place at the elementary and junior high school level. Some of the most interesting innovations have been made in college courses. The traditional college course includes a set of readings, lectures, and usually two or three exams. The exams are given at fixed times during the quarter or semester, and the students' grades depend upon their performance on the exams. They are held responsible for material covered both in the readings and in lectures. Typically, grades are normally distributed (fall within a bell-shaped normal curve). What this usually means is that only the students at the top end of the distribution have learned the material well.

Fred Keller (1968) suggested a number of innovations within the college classroom which would allow every student to master the material. The readings for the course were broken up into small units. The student had to pass an examination on one unit before proceeding to the next—and had to pass this material perfectly. The exam could be repeated if the student failed. Examinations were given by an undergraduate proctor (someone who had previously mastered the material and thus could serve as a tester as well as a source of information about the material). When the student was ready to take an exam, all that was necessary was to go to the proctor and ask for one. Examinations were completely individualized in that they were given only when the student was ready for them. The important point to note is that students could not proceed in the course unless they passed the examination perfectly for each unit. When a student failed an examination, the proctor would direct the student back to the appropriate parts of the readings. Since every student was required to get a perfect score on every test, grades represented how far into the course the student had penetrated. Thus a person who completed all units would get an A, a person who completed less than all the units would get a B, a C, and so forth. Keller also included a final examination which counted for 30 percent of the grade. Lectures and demonstrations were not compulsory and were not tested. Instead, they were used as reinforcement. A student was not allowed to go to a lecture without having passed the examinations that would make the material relevant. The features which most distinguished this method from traditional teaching procedures were summarized by Keller as follows:

1. The go-at-your-own-pace feature, *which permits a student to move through the course at a speed commensurate with his ability and other demands upon his time.*
2. The unit-perfection requirement for advance, *which lets the student go ahead to new material only after demonstrating mastery of that which preceded.*
3. The use of lectures and demonstrations as vehicles of motivation, *rather than sources of critical information.*
4. The related stress upon written word *in teacher-student communication;* and, finally:
5. The use of proctors, *which permits repeated testing, immediate scoring, almost unavoidable tutoring, and a marked enhancement of the personal-social aspect of the educational process.*

An experiment comparing this method of teaching with the conventional way was performed by James McMichael and Jeffery Corey (1969). One introductory psychology section having over two hundred students was taught using the Keller method and compared with three other sections using the same textbook but taught in a conventional manner with three or four examinations. All sections were given the same final examination. The test scores appear in Figure 3-6. As can be clearly seen in the figure, the experimental (contingency management) class far outperformed the traditional classes. In addition, the student ratings indicated that the experimental class was preferred to the traditional classes; students enjoyed it much more.

There seems to be little doubt that courses can in fact be structured so that everyone can master the material. It should be clear that this does not mean that the student works less. In fact, students frequently work much harder in courses such as this because the reinforcements are clear and predictable.

The Home

The point has been emphasized throughout this chapter that behavior is best changed in the setting in which it is a problem. There are many problems which occur in the home, and it is here that contingency management has its greatest potential. A good illustration of this was reported by H. Lal and Ogden Lindsley (1968). They described the case of a young child who was suffering from chronic constipation. A few days after birth, the child had de-

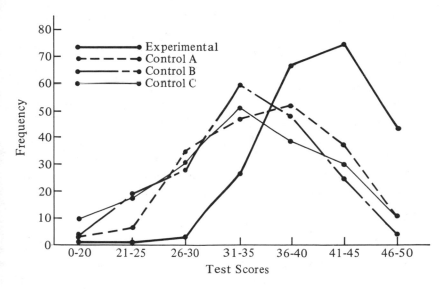

Figure 3-6
Distribution of test scores for the three control classes and the experimental class. The mean score for the experimental class was 40; for Control A, 35; Control B, 34; and Control C, 34. (From McMichael and Corey, 1969.)

veloped severe diarrhea which resulted in hospitalization and nearly three months of medical attention. After the diarrhea had been alleviated he developed constipation and remained constipated during the next three years. He rarely passed stools without a suppository laxative.

At the time the child was brought for treatment, his parents were following an elaborate daily ritual. The child was placed on the toilet seat for between one to two hours each day. If he became uncomfortable during this time, his mother entertained him to keep him there. If he started to cry, she soothed him. Once a week he received a suppository laxative and was placed on the toilet 1½ to two hours after receiving it. Invariably he defecated on the day of medication and occasionally on the following day.

After being told that the child particularly enjoyed taking a bath, instructions were given to the mother to alter the contingencies following defecation. The new consequences were to be started on a day the child was given a suppository. Before placing the child on the toilet seat, the mother was to fill the tub with water and place some of his favorite toys in it. She was to tell him that when he had finished going to the bathroom he could take a bath. Then, she was to leave the bathroom telling him to call her when he finished. The first trial was likely to be successful (i.e., end with the reinforcer being given) since previously the child had always defecated after being given a suppository. And, in fact, the first trial was successful. After the child called her, the mother found that he had defecated, so she allowed him to play in the bath tub. She followed the new routine without a suppository for the next two weeks. On each of these days the child defecated. At the end of two weeks she stopped reinforcing the passing of stools with playing in the bath tub, and the child successfully maintained his newly acquired elimination habits.

The gains made by the rather simple procedures of altering the social contingencies were remarkable. Yet it is unclear which contingencies were most important since a number of changes were made at the same time. The mother was told (1) to stop staying in the bathroom with her child, (2) to reinforce his success with social reinforcement, and (3) to reinforce success by allowing him to take a bath. It cannot be determined which of these factors was most important in this case from the information available. As scientists we would like to know which factor was crucial, but as therapists we want to maximize the possibility of improvement. What is particularly impressive about this study is that a condition which had been maintained for three years and had resisted medical treatment was easily altered in two weeks by instituting some minor changes in social contingencies.

TOILET TRAINING

Contingency management has also been suggested as a way of making toilet training of normal children less stressful and more efficient. Richard Foxx and Nathan Azrin (1973) have demonstrated that it is possible to toilet train normal children who are at least 20 months of age in one day! To do this they have devised an intensive learning procedure.

For the demonstration project children were recruited through a newspaper ad and by word of mouth. The children were then screened to be sure that they could follow verbal instructions. The final sample consisted of 34 children ranging in age from 20 to 36 months. Almost all of the parents complained of difficulties in toilet training their children.

Each child was trained individually in the child's home. Parents and family members were asked to leave for the day. The trainer in each instance was a female adult.

To increase the number of times the child would have to go to the bathroom, he was given fluids to drink about every five minutes (about two cups were consumed each hour). A list was obtained from the child's mother of the child's favorite drinks.

The trainer instructed the child, manually guided the child, and reinforced the successful completion of each component skill in the act of toileting. The components included approaching the already provided potty chair, lowering the pants, sitting on the potty chair, wiping oneself, getting up from the chair, raising the pants, removing the urine-filled pot from the chair, bringing the pot to the toilet, emptying the pot, flushing the toilet, and returning the pot to the chair. Reinforcement consisted of praise, hugs, special treats, and telling the children how pleased their parents, friends, and "heroes" would be.

Between toiletings, the child was given a doll which could be filled with water and was taught to carry out all the components of toileting with the doll.

However, the child might learn all the components of toileting without ever learning when to go to the toilet. Therefore, the trainer inspected the child's pants about every five minutes, and reinforced the child if the pants were dry. If the child's pants were wet, he was reprimanded. The trainer also omitted reinforcement at the next dry pants check, omitted social interaction for about five minutes, and then had the child change his pants. As the final consequence for wet pants, the child had to practice rapid toileting from different parts of the house for a total of 10 trials. During each trial, the child went to the potty chair, lowered his pants, stayed seated for about two seconds, stood up, raised his pants, and moved to the next location.

To provide practice in toileting, the child was told to go to the toilet about every 10 minutes, was allowed to sit on the potty chair for about 5 minutes unless he urinated before that. The child was reinforced for urinating.

Detailed instructions and reinforcement for each component were faded as the child progressed. Once the child toileted alone without prompting, the trainer no longer reminded the child to go to the toilet. Thereafter, one or two dry pants checks were made and little additional training was required.

As can be seen, many different procedures were being combined to teach appropriate toileting behavior to the child. When reading through the long list of activities, it seems rather overwhelming. Since the trainers were well practiced, it was not difficult for them and it was not a trying experience for the children. In fact, the children enjoyed the training. The large number of hugs and treats and large amount of praise made it a very enjoyable experience. In addition, the children seemed to get particular pleasure from playing with the doll, emptying the potty, and flushing the toilet. A few of the children were resistant and had tantrums at the beginning of training. This initial reluctance was overcome quickly when the children were given manual graduated guidance whenever they failed to respond to a request.

The average training period took four hours. The quickest was finished in a half-hour, while the longest took 14 hours. When the parents returned, they were delighted with the results. To ensure that the gains would be maintained, the parents were instructed to check the child's pants before meals, and at naps and bedtime. In case of accidents, the child was to be reprimanded, made to change his pants, and made to practice going to the toilet. This home monitoring was necessary only for the three or four days following training.

The week before training, the children averaged six accidents a day. After training, they averaged about one accident a week. This success was maintained through a four-month follow-up and was true for bowel movements as well as urination. Clearly this is a far superior procedure for toilet training children than those haphazard and frequently stressful techniques that parents often employ.

DEALING WITH MULTIPLE PROBLEMS

Not all problems for which contingency management is effective are as focused as toilet training. Contingency management offers possible solutions for problems affecting the person's total adjustment as well. For example, children referred to child guidance clinics usually have multiple problems which affect the child's adjustment both at home and in school. Contingency management programs could be developed for each separate problem in both settings. Gerald Patterson and G. Brodsky (1966) described the treatment of a five-year-old boy (Karl) who exhibited multiple problems at home and in school. At home, Karl refused both to be separated from his mother for any length of time and to perform self-care behaviors. When Karl did not get his way, he threw violent tantrums which included screaming, biting, kicking, and throwing anything that was nearby. In school, Karl also threw tantrums, and he was frequently aggressive toward other children and the teacher. "The teacher's legs were a mass of black and blue marks; on several occasions he had tried to throttle her." Karl's behavior in kindergarten had become so unmanageable that his parents were asked to remove him.

To deal with Karl's many problems, Patterson and Brodsky developed four different programs. The first program dealt with tantrums; the second dealt with being separated from mother; the third attempted to increase the frequency of positive interactions between Karl and other children; and the fourth was a program to teach Karl's parents to reinforce independent behaviors at home.

Since Karl threw a tantrum every time he was separated from his mother, it was easy to start a program for extinguishing tantrums. Karl was brought by his mother to a mobile trailer which was divided into two rooms. Karl was taken into one of them (carried if necessary) and then allowed to have his tantrum. To prevent Karl from destroying the room, the therapist pinned Karl's feet to the floor by holding his ankles. The therapist continued this, looking as bored as possible, until Karl stopped screaming. The next day the same procedure was followed and Karl quieted down within a few minutes. After Karl had calmed down, the program dealing with separation from mother was begun. This consisted of having Karl play a doll game in which the mother doll was separated from the boy doll. Karl was asked if the doll would be afraid. If he answered that it would not be afraid, he was given an M&M candy. Thus, he was reinforced for verbal statements indicating tolerance for separation. Karl earned about 30 M&Ms a session.

Karl's mother watched the sessions through a one-way mirror and was told to watch how the therapist reinforced Karl's appropriate behavior and ignored inappropriate behavior. In addition, she was given the assignment of reinforcing Karl at home whenever he behaved independently. At the end of each session, the therapists, Karl, and his mother met and reviewed the mother's report of the previous day's reinforcements. The mother mentioned all the things that Karl did that were independent and the way she reinforced them. This public demonstration of Karl's independent behavior seemed to please him considerably. The therapists next arranged to visit Karl and his parents at their home. They followed both parents around and made suggestions from time to time on appropriate ways of handling Karl. Most of their suggestions focused on opportunities to reinforce independent and appropriate behavior.

The program to increase interaction between Karl and other children took place during the recess period at school. The therapists brought a box which they called the "Karl box" that contained a counter, light, and loud bell. When the bell went off, the counter would click and the therapist would give Karl an M&M. During recess time, Karl was told that the bell would sound each time that he "played with another kid without hurting him." He also was told that any candy that he earned would be divided among all the children and distributed at snack time. Thus, not only was Karl being reinforced for talking to his classmates, but they were being reinforced for talking to Karl.

Two weeks after the treatment programs began, they were terminated. Karl had shown such dramatic improvement that further treatment was unnecessary, and follow-up observations indicated that the improvement was maintained.

Perhaps the most significant aspect of this study is the extent to which Patterson and Brodsky went to ensure that the other children responded positively to changes made by Karl. They recognized that it was the consequences provided by other children which would be crucial in maintaining Karl's appropriate social behavior.

Another aspect of the study that should be stressed is the training of the parents. Karl's parents were taught how to be more effective contingency managers. They were able to alter their own behavior so as to reinforce independence in Karl. Often, parents with problem children are overwhelmed with feelings of guilt and inadequacy because of their child-rearing failures. Many investigators have found that parents begin to view themselves more positively as they experience success with contingency management.

BEHAVIORAL CONTRACTS

Karl was quite young and still interested in receiving M&Ms. A much more difficult problem confronts society in dealing with "delinquent" adolescents. Institutionalization is seldom effective and is a drastic consequence when the "crime" the adolescent has committed is often only failure to attend school, running away from home, or violations of parental authority. Thus, it would be desirable to have an effective means of altering the family environment so that prosocial behavior could be encouraged before the State was required to intervene. Richard Stuart (1971) has suggested that behavioral contracts provide just such a means of altering the family environment.

A behavioral contract is an agreement that states what consequences will follow certain behaviors. Table 3-2 is an illustration of one particular contract. According to Stuart, there are five elements in a good behavioral contract. First, the contract must be explicit about the benefits or privileges each person will receive as a result of fulfilling his or her responsibilities. Second, it must be possible to monitor whether activities required by the contract are actually completed. Third, there must be a system of sanctions for failure to meet the terms of the contract. Fourth, there should be bonuses for compliance with the terms of the contract. This point is important because it gives the family an additional opportunity to positively reinforce appropriate behavior instead of relying upon punishment. The fifth and final element is that there should be a record-keeping system so that it will be clear exactly when a benefit is earned. It should also be emphasized that it is essential that all parties have agreed to abide by the contract.

The sample contract in Table 3-2 contains all the elements listed above; but why should Candy agree to such a contract? Candy Bremer (not her real name) was a 16-year-old girl who at the time Stuart became involved had already been hospitalized in a private psychiatric hospital following alleged "promiscuity, exhibitionism, drug abuse and home truancy." Her parents also complained that she constantly fought with them and was close to failing in school. Because the private hospital was too expensive, Mr. and Mrs. Bremer (who were both physically ill and 64 and 61 years old, respectively) initially petitioned the juvenile court to assume wardship so that Candy could be hospitalized at state expense. After some negotiation, the Bremers reluctantly allowed Candy to stay with them only if she would adhere to a very severe curfew which allowed her out of the house an average of two to three hours a day during the summer. Within three weeks Candy was sneaking out of her window at night to visit a local commune and would return before dawn. The contract in Table 3-2 was then instituted, and a

Table 3-2
Behavioral Contract

PRIVILEGES	RESPONSIBILITIES
General	
In exchange for the privilege of remaining together and preserving some semblance of family integrity, Mr. and Mrs. Bremer and Candy all agree to	
	concentrate on positively reinforcing each other's behavior while diminishing the present overemphasis upon the faults of the others.
Specific	
In exchange for the privilege of riding the bus directly from school into town after school on school days	
	Candy agrees to phone her father by 4:00 P.M. to tell him that she is all right and to return home by 5:15 P.M.
In exchange for the privilege of going out at 7:00 P.M. on one weekend evening without having to account for her whereabouts	
	Candy must maintain a weekly average of "B" in the academic ratings of all of her classes and must return home by 11:30 P.M.
In exchange for the privilege of going out a second weekend night	
	Candy must tell her parents *by 6:00 P.M.* of her destination and her companion, and must return home by 11:30 P.M.

PRIVILEGES	RESPONSIBILITIES
In exchange for the privilege of going out between 11:00 A.M. and 5:15 P.M. Saturdays, Sundays and holidays	
	Candy agrees to have completed all household chores *before* leaving and to telephone her parents once during the time she is out to tell them that she is all right.
In exchange for the privilege of having Candy complete household chores and maintain her curfew	
	Mr. and Mrs. Bremer agree to pay Candy $1.50 on the morning following days on which the money is earned.
Bonuses and Sanctions If Candy is 1–10 minutes late	
	she must come in the same amount of time earlier the following day, but she does not forfeit her money for the day.
If Candy is 11–30 minutes late	
	she must come in 22–60 minutes earlier the following day and does forfeit her money for the day.
If Candy is 31–60 minutes late	
	she loses the privilege of going out the following day and does forfeit her money for the day.
For each half hour of tardiness over one hour, Candy	
	loses her privilege of going out and her money for one additional day.
Candy may go out on Sunday evenings from 7:00 to 9:30 P.M. and either Monday or Thursday evening	

Table 3-2
Behavioral Contract (cont.)

PRIVILEGES	RESPONSIBILITIES
	if she abides by all the terms of this contract from Sunday through Saturday with a total tardiness not exceeding 30 minutes which must have been made up as above.
Candy may add a total of two hours divided among one to three curfews	
	if she abides by all the terms of this contract for two weeks with a total tardiness not exceeding 30 minutes which must have been made up as above and if she requests permission to use this additional time by 9:00 P.M.

MONITORING

Mr. and Mrs. Bremer agree to keep written records of the hours of Candy's leaving and coming home and of the completion of her chores.

Candy agrees to furnish her parents with a school monitoring card each Friday at dinner.

From Stuart, 1971.

court order issued stating that if Candy were found in the commune the commune members could be prosecuted for contributing to the delinquency of a minor.

Given this background, it is obvious that Candy could benefit enormously from the contract. She could go out on weekends, earn additional time away from home, and get an allowance. In addition, these benefits could not be withdrawn because of a parental whim—if she earned them they were hers. The Bremers would also benefit. Candy had to keep them informed, do reasonably well in school, complete her chores, and be home on time. These were the things they were concerned about. The contract would also reduce the frequency of arguments about privileges and responsibilities.

After the contract was instituted, Candy met its requirements a very high proportion of the time. Even after the court wardship was terminated, Candy's behavior continued to improve.

Behavioral contracts may not be sufficient in every instance; however, they provide a useful tool to help improve interactions between adolescents and their parents.

A comprehensive program using behavioral contracts has been developed and evaluated by Patterson (1974). Patterson's procedure gradually evolved through the process of treating individual cases (including the previously described case of Karl). The complete program was then applied to 27 consecutive referrals of boys with conduct problems. These boys had extensive, long-term histories of conduct problems and were referred from community agencies such as their schools, juvenile court, and mental health clinics.

The program focused primarily on training the parents. First, parents studied a programmed text on child management techniques (either Patterson and Guillion, 1968, or Patterson, 1971). Second, they learned to define and record specific deviant and prosocial behaviors. Third, they participated in a parent-training group where modeling and role playing were used to help teach the techniques. And fourth, they learned to construct behavioral contracts with their children.

Behavioral observations were made by trained observers in the home before, during, and after the intervention. Reports from the parents were also received daily. The results indicated that deviant behavior decreased considerably during the training period and improvement was maintained through a 12-month follow-up.

This study is particularly important since all boys referred were accepted for treatment. It is not the case that techniques only work with certain highly focused problem behaviors. Rather, these techniques are also effective if the boys have multiple problems and long histories of difficulty.

Future Directions

Contingency management has been applied in other settings besides the ones reviewed in this chapter (e.g., in prisons, institutions for retarded children, and homes for juvenile delinquents). The advantages and practical difficulties are much the same as those already discussed. In some cases, programs within these settings raise additional ethical and legal questions. This is particularly true for programs within prisons, where there is often justifiable concern that prison-sponsored programs might jeopardize prisoners' basic rights.

Additional controversy is centered on whether prisoners can ever truly give their informed consent to participate in a prison-sponsored program. The fear is that prisoners might volunteer for programs in which they do not truly wish to participate in hope of favored treatment or out of fear of reprisals. These issues, along with other philosophical and ethical problems, will be more fully explored in Chapter 6.

Potentially, contingency management principles could be used to solve a number of pressing social problems. B. F. Skinner (1948) in his book *Walden II* speculated about what an entire society might be like if developed according to operant principles. Not everything in that society may be achievable, or even desirable; however, there is room for much improvement in our society and the application of contingency management principles may help in that direction.

Recommended Readings

AYLLON, T., & AZRIN, N. *The token economy: A motivational system for therapy and rehabilitation.* New York: Appleton-Century-Crofts, 1968. *This is a detailed description of Ayllon and Azrin's token economy within a mental hospital. It contains some invaluable practical suggestions as well.*

KAZDIN, A. E., & BOOTZIN, R. R. The token economy: An evaluative review. *Journal of Applied Behavior Analysis,* 1972, *5,* 343-372. *This is a review of the literature for studies employing token economies with psychiatric patients, retardates, children in classroom settings, delinquents, and autistic children. Methodological problems are also discussed.*

ULRICH, R., STACHNIK, T., & MABRY, J. (Eds.). *Control of human behavior.* Vols. 1 and 2. Glenview, Ill.: Scott, Foresman, 1966, 1970. *These two books of readings contain many of the articles referred to in this chapter as well as others related to contingency management.*

4

Counterconditioning and Extinction

Studies of learning can be roughly divided into two broad categories
—classical conditioning and instrumental conditioning. The basic
paradigm for classical conditioning is a previously neutral stimulus
(the conditioned stimulus) paired with a stimulus that reflexively
elicits a response (the unconditioned stimulus). By repeated pairing,
the neutral stimulus becomes conditioned to elicit a response similar
to the one elicited by the unconditioned stimulus. Figure 4-1 dia-
grams this process. The experimenter presents the unconditioned
stimulus independently of the subject's performance.

In contrast, in instrumental conditioning the experimenter
presents the unconditioned stimulus (the reinforcement) only after
the subject makes an appropriate response. The subject's behavior
determines whether or not the unconditioned stimulus is presented.
If the subject does not emit the appropriate response, the reinforcement is not delivered. *Classical conditioning changes the stimulus
value of the neutral stimulus while instrumental conditioning focuses
on changing the response pattern.*

The experiment with Little Albert and the laboratory rat described in Chapter 1 is a good example of classical conditioning.
The rat (a previously neutral, in fact slightly positive, stimulus)
was repeatedly paired with a loud noise until the rat elicited a fear
response similar to that elicited by the noise. The goal of the procedure was to alter the stimulus value of the laboratory rat. On the
other hand, the contingency management studies are good examples

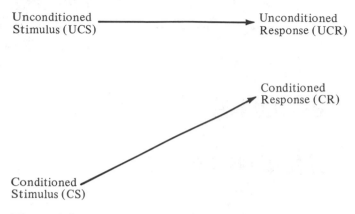

Figure 4-1
Model of classical conditioning.

of instrumental conditioning (or what B. F. Skinner calls operant conditioning). The consequences of a response were altered in order to increase or decrease its frequency.

The previous chapters have described techniques based primarily upon instrumental or operant conditioning principles. In contrast, the focus of the present chapter will be upon approaches derived from classical conditioning principles.

Mary Cover Jones (1924) was the first to use classical conditioning systematically to eliminate children's fears. She studied the effectiveness of numerous techniques, but with one child (Peter) she tried a conditioning procedure. Peter, 2 years 10 months old, was afraid of rabbits. The conditioning procedure involved pairing the stimulus to be conditioned (the rabbit) with the unconditioned stimulus (food). During Peter's usual mid-morning snack, a rabbit was brought as close to Peter as he would tolerate. If he started to show any discomfort, the rabbit was moved as far away as necessary for Peter to start eating his candy again. Then, while Peter was eating, the rabbit was again moved closer. This procedure was followed daily or twice daily until Peter was comfortable in the presence of the rabbit. The laboratory notes for the first training trial read:

Case 30.—Peter. Age 2 years, 10 months.
March 10, 10:15 A.M. Peter sitting in high chair, eating candy. Experimenter entered room with a rabbit in an open-meshed wire cage. The rabbit was placed on the table 4 feet from Peter who

immediately began to cry, insisting that the rabbit be taken away. Continued crying until the rabbit was put down 20 feet away. He then started again on the candy, but continued to fuss, "I want you to put Bunny outside." After 3 minutes he once more burst into tears; the rabbit was removed.

Seven weeks later, at the last training trial, Peter's behavior was much different.

April 29, 9:55 A.M. Peter standing in high chair, looking out of the window. He inquired, "Where is the rabbit?" The rabbit was put down on the chair at Peter's feet. Peter patted him, tried to pick him up, but finding the rabbit was too heavy asked the experimenter to help in lifting him to the window sill, where he played with him for several minutes (Jones, 1924, p. 389).

It is evident that the conditioning procedure reduced Peter's fear of the rabbit. However, in Jones's procedure the rabbit was a rather unusual conditioned stimulus. Although it had been repeatedly associated with food, Peter did not start salivating at the sight of it. Instead, what appears to have occurred is that Peter had been conditioned to associate the rabbit with the "pleasure" accompanying eating.

Although this case demonstrated that conditioning procedures had considerable promise for reducing fear, there were only scattered attempts to explore conditioning techniques further during the next 30 years. One of these attempts, an extensive project to treat alcoholics, will be discussed in the next chapter.

In the 1950s a number of researchers in England, South Africa, and the United States began again to explore the possibilities of developing conditioning procedures for reducing anxiety and other "symptoms." The work of Joseph Wolpe, who was then in South Africa, served as a major impetus for the development of behavior therapy.

Systematic Desensitization

Joseph Wolpe (1958) developed a number of counterconditioning approaches for the reduction of anxiety. The goal of these procedures is to weaken the association between certain environmental cues and the patient's responses of anxiety. This is done by repeatedly exposing the patient to fear-evoking cues under conditions which prevent the arousal of anxiety. Anxiety arousal is prevented by having the patient engage in incompatible behavior, such as relaxation, assertive behavior, or sexual behavior. Wolpe's technique using relaxation is called systematic desensitization and has been more widely used than the other techniques. As a result, it has a proportionately larger research literature. It has three components: (1) anxiety hierarchy construction, (2) relaxation training, and (3) scene presentation during relaxation.

Hierarchy construction. An anxiety hierarchy is a series of anxiety-producing scenes which the client has arranged from most to least anxiety-producing. Here is the hierarchy constructed by a female student who complained of examination anxiety (Wolpe, 1973):

1. On the way to the university on the day of an examination.
2. In the process of answering an examination paper.
3. Before the unopened doors of the examination room.
4. Awaiting the distribution of examination papers.
5. The examination paper lies face down before her.
6. The night before an examination.
7. One day before an examination.
8. Two days before an examination.
9. Three days before an examination.
10. Four days before an examination.
11. Five days before an examination.
12. A week before an examination.
13. Two weeks before an examination.
14. A month before an examination.

Notice that going to the examination was rated as more stressful (and thus was higher on the hierarchy) than actually taking the exam. This is not an infrequent occurrence. The anticipation of an event is often experienced as more stressful than the event itself.

Although hierarchies vary considerably, the items within a hierarchy usually have a common theme. Some hierarchies are very specific, dealing with such themes as anxiety associated with heights, injections, airplanes, and snakes. Other hierarchies deal with very complex interpersonal anxieties such as those associated with being rejected, being the center of attention, failure, and sex. Compulsions are treated by constructing hierarchies which deal with the anxiety produced by not carrying out the compulsion (e.g., having the urge to wash your hands, but not doing it). If a patient has many problems, a different hierarchy might be constructed for each problem.

Not all patients are able to identify the situations in which they feel anxious. In these instances the therapist helps the patient learn to discriminate the situations in which he is anxious. This may be accomplished by teaching the patient which physiological reactions ordinarily indicate anxiety and by having the patient monitor his reactions outside the consulting office.

Relaxation training. During the early sessions of the therapy, while hierarchies are being constructed, the patient is also instructed on how to achieve deep muscle relaxation using an abbreviated form of Jacobson's relaxation technique (see Chapter 2). Whereas Jacobson often took months to train a patient to relax, relaxation taught for the purpose of systematic desensitization usually takes two or three training sessions. First, to aid the patient in learning to discriminate relaxation from tension, the patient is asked to flex and release a number of different muscle groups. In subsequent sessions, he is asked to relax without flexing the muscles. Patients are instructed to practice relaxing between therapy sessions until they are able to achieve deep relaxation quickly. A patient having difficulty relaxing particular muscles is given additional training focused on them. Thus, a person who cannot relax the forehead may be given extra training on relaxing the muscles in the forehead, or a person who reports particular problems in relaxing neck muscles may be given extra training in relaxing those muscles.

Pairing of relaxation and anxiety scenes. After the patient has become proficient at achieving deep relaxation and after anxiety hierarchies have been constructed, the major portion of the therapy begins. First the patient is asked to achieve as deep a relaxed state as possible. Then, the lowest scene on the hierarchy is presented and the patient is asked to imagine it for about 10 seconds. If at any time the patient feels the least bit uncomfortable or anxious while imagining this scene, he is instructed to signal by raising the index finger of one hand. If the patient does signal, the scene is immediately terminated (the patient is asked to stop imagining it and to relax) and after a period of relaxation the patient is asked to imagine the same scene again. The patient proceeds to the next scene on the hierarchy only after achieving the ability to imagine the previous scene without feeling anxious. Thus, scenes to which the patient signals anxiety are repeated until they can be imagined without anxiety.

In both systematic desensitization and the procedure used by Mary Cover Jones with Peter, the anxiety-producing stimulus is introduced gradually in the presence of cues associated with responses other than anxiety (relaxation and eating, respectively). Jones presented the actual feared stimulus, while during systematic desensitization the patient usually imagines the feared stimulus. When the actual feared stimuli are presented, rather than imagined scenes, the procedure is called *in vivo* (taking place in real life) *desensitization. In vivo* desensitization and its variations will be discussed later in this chapter.

The rationale for the effectiveness of systematic desensitization is that by repeatedly associating scenes which normally arouse anxiety with deep muscle relaxation, the imagined scenes become counterconditioned ("desensitized"). The next scene in the hierarchy, then, can be more easily counterconditioned because of stimulus generalization from the previous scene. Although only the anxiety produced by imagined scenes is being counterconditioned, it has been generally assumed that there is a good correspondence between advancement up the hierarchy and behavioral improvements in other settings.

CASE STUDIES

Phobia. Two case studies will be presented here to give an idea of how systematic desensitization is ordinarily used. James Geer (1964) reported the use of systematic desensitization with a 17-year-old girl who had a phobia of lice. She was afraid lice would get in her hair through contact with other people. Apparently, a year and a half prior to treatment, she had contracted a case of lice which had been treated successfully by her mother. About one month later she began to develop a fear of getting another case of lice, and it was so intense that it severely interfered with her social life. In fact, she avoided going anywhere in public since there was always a chance of coming into contact with people who had lice. She was given a battery of psychological tests and these were interpreted as indicating that she "is irritable, nervous, tense, lonely, and unhappy. She is fearful, suspicious, and depressed. Although her anxiety seems at present focused on a strong fear of bugs, it is much more pervasive than this and extends throughout all aspects of her life."

The first five treatment sessions were devoted to practicing relaxation and constructing an anxiety hierarchy, which was as follows (Geer, 1964):

1. A stranger notices a tangle in your hair and tries to help you by combing it out with her comb. (11)
2. Your sister is fixing your hair when she drops the curlers on the floor, picks them up, and uses them in your hair. (11)
3. A stranger in the washroom at school hands you her comb and asks you to hold it for her. (10)
4. While standing looking at an ad in a store window, someone comes up beside you and puts their head near yours to see too. (10)
5. A stranger asks to use your comb and continues to ask why not when you say no. (9)
6. You are combing your hair in the washroom when someone asks to borrow your comb. (9)
7. While sitting in the local snack bar a friend tells you of her experiences when she had a case of lice. (8 and 9)
8. While sitting at home with your sister, she tells you that she used someone else's comb today. (7 and 8)
9. A girl sitting in front of you in school leans her head back on your books. (6 and 7)
10. You are in a beauty shop having your hair set. (6)
11. In a public washroom you touch the seat of a commode. (6)
12. A girl puts her scarf on your lap. (5)
13. At school, in hygiene class, the teacher lectures on lice and bugs in people's hair. (4 and 5)
14. You are watching a movie and they show a scene where people are being deloused. (4, 5, and 6)
15. At a store you are asked to try on a wig and you comply. (3)
16. You are in a department store, and the saleslady is fitting a hat on you. (3)
17. You look at your desk top and notice several bobby pins and clips upon it. (3)
18. You are reading a *Reader's Digest* article that goes into detail concerning the catching and curing of a case of lice. (2)

19. You are at home watching television when an ad concerning dandruff removing shampoo comes on. (2)
20. While walking down the sidewalk you notice a comb in the gutter. (1)
21. While reading in school you notice a small bug on your book. (1)
22. Writing the words bug and lice. (1)

The items of the hierarchy were counterconditioned during the next 11 sessions. The numbers in parentheses indicate the number of the session at which the item was presented. Thus, the bottom three items were successfully counterconditioned during the first desensitization session. Each item was repeated until the subject could visualize it without experiencing anxiety for three successive presentations.

As the therapy proceeded, the subject reported that she was able to engage in activities that she had previously avoided. During session 8 she reported that she was spending less time thinking about her fear. During session 10, she mentioned that she had read about lice in school without experiencing anxiety. She also mentioned that a boy had stretched back in his seat and placed his head on her book; this did not bother her whereas previously she would have been very upset. One week after the last session, "the patient reported that the fear had diminished a considerable extent and that it no longer interfered with normal behavior. She did not report that it had completely disappeared, but only that it was no longer a source of concern to her." Three months later she was again contacted for a follow-up interview. She reported that she had improved even further. As an example, she reported that her new boyfriend had run his comb through her hair. She was only momentarily anxious about it and the anxiety quickly disappeared. There was no evidence of symptom substitution. In fact, the patient reported that there were favorable changes in her relationships with others and in many other aspects of her life. It is of course impossible to state whether these positive changes were due to the therapy itself. Most likely, however, as the patient became less and less concerned about catching lice her relationships with other people improved.

Social anxiety. A second illustration of systematic desensitization is its use for social anxieties (Bootzin, 1968). Majid, a 21-year-old foreign student from northern Africa, sought treatment because he felt anxious and compelled to vomit in a number of social situations. He was unable to meet and talk to strangers without vomiting. Although he felt comfortable with people who knew of his difficulty, he restricted his social activities considerably and did not date. However, he continued to go to his classes. Only his speech course presented any special difficulty. For this course, Majid was required to give a number of speeches in front of the rest of the class. To avoid vomiting during a speech, he would induce vomiting immediately before class began by sticking his finger down his throat.

Majid's problem had begun the previous year while he was home in Africa for summer vacation. About four weeks before he was to return to the United States, he started vomiting in social situations. Usually these were situations in which he was required to meet people and tell them about his experiences in the United States. He sought medical help both in Africa and in the United States. No organic basis for his problem was found. One physician suggested that it was a temporary problem, probably due to the difference in weather between the two locations. When the problem persisted, tranquilizers were prescribed without effect. Majid sought psychological counseling as a last resort. He was very pessimistic about his chances for improvement because he felt that his problem was physiological. In fact, he resisted talking about his family background because he saw no relationship between "psychological" events and his "physiological" problem. When the procedure for systematic desensitization was described he agreed to try it, but he remained very skeptical of the likelihood of success.

The first two treatment sessions after the intake interview were devoted to teaching Majid progressive relaxation and developing rough forms of four hierarchies. The four areas were (1) taking exams, (2) meeting strangers socially, (3) dating, and (4) giving speeches. Although Majid never vomited while taking an exam he did report that he was quite anxious about examinations, and it was felt that this might be a good place to start. Desensitization proper took place in the next five sessions. Majid was able to relax quite well, and progress through the hierarchies proceeded quickly. At the second desensitization session, he reported that he had not vomited for the previous two weeks. He considered this to be quite an accomplishment. However, at the next session, he reported having had to vomit. An old friend whom he had not seen for some time visited him. Majid talked to him for about 10 minutes and then, feeling compelled to vomit, excused himself, vomited, returned, and continued the conversation. At the fourth desensitization session, Majid reported that his roommates had given a party. He was sociable and comfortable even though there were many people he did not know. At the fifth session (the last session for desensitization proper) he reported that he had had a considerable number of social contacts without experiencing any difficulty. He anticipated no more problems even though he had to take a couple of exams and give a speech during the next week.

Majid came back the next week for the first follow-up session to report how the speech and exams had gone. He said that although he was a little anxious when the speech began, as he continued he felt very relaxed. At no time did he feel an urge to vomit. He was quite elated about his performance. He also reported taking his exams without being anxious.

A second follow-up was arranged six weeks later, which coincided with Majid's return to campus after the spring vacation. At this time he reported that he had not vomited since last seen. During spring vacation he went on a bus trip with 30 other students. He led the bus in community singing and toured most of the stops with one of the women on the trip. He was obviously no longer keeping himself socially isolated. The only occasion when he felt at all anxious was when he had to call his government's consul. However, on that occasion he did not have an urge to vomit but, in contrast, felt that his anxiety was completely under control. Majid was seen for a one-year follow-up, at which time he again reported that he had not vomited since the previous meeting.

The Effectiveness of Systematic Desensitization

There are many case studies, such as those above, reporting the successful application of systematic desensitization to a wide variety of problems. These include isolated phobias, interpersonal anxiety, sexual frigidity, compulsions, and insomnia. Joseph Wolpe (1958) reported that 89 percent of his clients, including those treated with techniques other than systematic desensitization, were much improved after treatment. An estimate of his success rates for clients receiving primarily systematic desensitization is 92 percent (Paul, 1969a). Other therapists (e.g., Lazarus, 1963) have reported similarly high success rates. Even more remarkable than the high percentage of success is the small number of treatment sessions. The median number of sessions per client receiving systematic desensitization from Wolpe is 23 sessions. If the sessions are divided by the number of hierarchies per patient, the median number of sessions per hierarchy is 8 (the median number of hierarchies per patient is 2). Twenty-three sessions is a remarkably short time compared to more traditional psychotherapies, such as psychoanalysis, during which the patient accumulates hundreds of sessions over a period of years.

The case reports of the success of systematic desensitization for such a variety of anxiety-related problems helped generate interest in the technique. However, case studies are not good evidence. Even if we are sure that the patient's behavior improved, we cannot be certain that improvement was due to the treatment. There are a number of other possibilities. For example, perhaps Majid stopped vomiting because of physiological changes associated with the passage of time; or perhaps he received an *A* on an exam which made him feel so good that it set off processes that caused his improvement; or perhaps he changed his eating habits and that caused the improvement. Any number of things might have been associated accidentally with the beginning of treatment. Case studies can never rule out coincidence as an alternative explanation.

Case studies also cannot rule out treatment-produced coincidences. The therapist reassures the patient; the patient expects to improve; the patient has identified himself as having a problem; and so forth. These, rather than treatment procedures, may be the important elements of the therapy.

So far in this discussion of case studies, we have assumed that we were convinced that the patient's behavior had, in fact, improved. However, there are problems associated with measuring improvement as well. Most case studies (including those reported by Wolpe and Lazarus) rely upon the therapist's rating of the patient's reports of improvement. There are many potential sources of error here. First, the *patient* may be biasing reports to the therapist. A patient trying to enlist the therapist's aid may exaggerate the extent of his difficulty. Then, when the patient wishes to terminate therapy, he may exaggerate his improvement. Even if a therapist had provided no treatment, the patient would appear to have improved. This pattern of biased reporting has been called the "hello-goodbye" effect.

Because success in behavior therapy is defined as symptom alleviation, there is often no need to rely so heavily on the patient's verbal report. A patient treated for fear of heights could be taken to the top of a tall building and asked to count the people passing below, a patient treated for fear of snakes could be asked to hold one, and so forth. The behavioral measures of improvement are not likely to be as easily biased as the subject's report of improvement. Unfortunately, most case studies (even those from behavior therapists) still rely solely upon the patient's report.

A second major source of error in the usual measures of improvement is that the *therapist* does the interviewing. Therapists are hardly disinterested observers. Even with the best of intentions, it is possible that they inadvertently will bias the results in their own favor.

If case studies have so many defects, what good are they? Should they be published at all? The history of most areas, particularly within behavior change, shows progress from poorly controlled case studies to methodologically sophisticated experiments. The interest and enthusiasm that starts such a chain of research is often generated by a case study. Many areas would not have been researched at all had it not been for the accumulation of successful case studies.

Experimental evidence. What procedures are necessary to rule out the competing explanations of maturation, extraneous events, and nonspecific therapy effects? The best procedure would be to include various groups of control subjects, some who do not receive the treatment at all. If treated subjects improve and the control subjects do not, we have effectively ruled out maturation and coincidence. Then the crucial elements of the treatment could be identified by having additional subjects receive different parts of the procedure. However, subjects often are a scarce commodity. There may be very few people suffering from a particular problem, perhaps too few to assign to control groups.

A strategy which requires only one subject and yet is a vast improvement over the case study is the within-subject ABA design (the *A* refers to the treatment, and the *B* refers to the reversal or withdrawal of treatment). Instead of using a control group, each subject goes through control periods. If the subject improves every time a treatment begins, and relapses every time a treatment is withdrawn, we can rule out maturation and coincidence and confidently conclude that the treatment causes improvement. This type of design has been used frequently to evaluate contingency management procedures (see Chapter 3) but seldom has been used for evaluating systematic desensitization.

The controlled studies of systematic desensitization have instead used randomly assigned control subjects. One of the best of these studies was carried out by Gordon Paul (1966) with speech-anxious college students. This study will be described in detail to illustrate how competing hypotheses can be controlled.

Of the 380 students who volunteered, the 96 most anxious were selected. Before treatment started, all subjects gave a speech before an unfamiliar audience under standard conditions. This provided a way to obtain behavioral and physiological data associated with giving speeches, in addition to the usual verbal reports. Subjects were randomly assigned to one of five groups: (1) systematic desensitization, (2) insight-oriented psychotherapy, (3) attention-placebo treatment, (4) waiting-list control, and (5) no-contact control. The waiting-list control subjects received all assessments but did not receive the treatment. The no-contact control subjects did not receive the special screening or subsequent assessments. They were not even aware that they were part of the study. Their progress was assessed by means of questionnaires given to students in the public speaking course from which all subjects were drawn.

Five psychotherapists, representatives of traditional insight-oriented schools of psychotherapy and having from 6 to 18 years of experience, were recruited to participate in the study. When asked to estimate how many sessions would be required to treat speech anxiety using their own therapies, they replied that five hour-long sessions would be sufficient. On this basis, all treatment groups were limited to five sessions. Each therapist expected his own therapy to be more effective than systematic desensitization.

Each therapist treated three subjects with his own insight therapy, three with systematic desensitization, and three with an attention-placebo treatment. The attention-placebo treatment was included to control for the possibility that experiencing any believable treatment would have beneficial effects. For this treatment, subjects received a bogus tranquilizer and were told to signal whenever they heard a certain sound. Subjects were told that if they had not taken a tranquilizer, this task would be very stressful, and that practice in dealing with stress while relaxed would generalize to other stressful situations. In fact, the task was boring, and no beneficial effects could theoretically have been expected. If subjects did improve, it would most likely be due to the subject's expectancy and other nonspecific therapy effects.

The results indicated that systematic desensitization was superior to all other groups on verbal report, on behavioral measures during the test speech, and on pulse rates and galvanic skin response taken immediately before a test speech. The attention-placebo and the insight-oriented treatment groups were better than the no-treatment control groups on the verbal and behavioral measures but not on the physiological measures.

Six-week and two-year follow-ups were undertaken to test the long-term effects of the treatments. After two years, 85 percent of those receiving systematic desensitization showed improvement from pretreatment to posttreatment, as compared with 50 percent of the insight psychotherapy group, 50 percent of the attention-placebo group, and 22 percent of the untreated controls. Gains made during the treatment were maintained, and there was no evidence of symptom substitution. This study more than any other clearly demonstrated the superiority of systematic desensitization over traditional insight-oriented psychotherapies in dealing with anxiety associated with specific stimuli.

Gordon Paul (1969b, p. 159) reviewed the studies investigating the effectiveness of systematic desensitization. His review of 75 articles involving about a thousand different patients treated by over 90 different therapists led him to conclude that

> the findings were overwhelmingly positive, and for the first time in the history of psychological treatments, a specific therapeutic package reliably produced measurable benefits for clients across a broad range of distressing problems in which anxiety was of fundamental importance.

THE ROLE OF EXPECTANCY IN SYSTEMATIC DESENSITIZATION

In Paul's study, the attention-placebo treatment was included as a way of controlling for subjects' expectancy of improvement. Since systematic desensitization was more effective than the attention-placebo group, Paul concluded that systematic desensitization was more than just an expectancy manipulation. However, since the attention-placebo group did show some improvement which was maintained at the two-year follow-up, it seems that expectancy manipulations themselves might be further investigated as viable techniques for changing phobic behavior. There is already a large literature indicating that expectancies are important determinants of other behavior. For example, within drug research the power of expectancy is attested to by the common use of sugar pills (placebos). It would not be surprising then if expectancy were an important variable in altering phobic behavior as well. It might even be possible to devise a placebo treatment which would be so convincing that it would be as effective as systematic desensitization.

James Marcia, Barry Rubin, and Jay Efran (1969) seem to have developed the even better placebo treatment. Snake- and spider-fearful subjects were told that they would be viewing pictures of the phobic object flashed so rapidly that the pictures could not be seen by the conscious mind but would be detected by the unconscious. In addition, unconscious responses would be monitored by physiological equipment and when a certain number of responses were detected, the subject would receive an electric shock to suppress them. The noteworthy addition to the treatment is that the subject was shown false polygraph printouts indicating that the subject's physiological responses were decreasing across sessions. To provide further feedback, the number of shocks the subject received also decreased.

The results showed that subjects receiving this placebo treatment improved as much as subjects receiving systematic desensitization. However, their major measure was a behavioral approach test using a *preserved* snake or spider. Bandura (1969) has pointed out that inhibitions aroused by a dead specimen may be considerably weaker and easier to manipulate than those aroused by a live animal. In addition, the subjects were college students who, although fearful, were probably not phobic. It may be that expectancy manipulations are effective only with less fearful subjects.

To follow up on these possibilities, John Lick (in press) executed a more carefully controlled study. Through newspaper ads, he solicited people in the Chicago area who were extremely fearful of snakes or spiders, and he used a live boa constrictor and a live tarantula during the approach tests. Subjects were given a maximum of eight sessions of therapy.

Lick found that the expectancy treatment was as effective as systematic desensitization even using a very fearful (probably phobic) population. However, subjects were limited to eight sessions of treatment, which meant that many systematic desensitization subjects did not finish the hierarchy. Nevertheless, Lick's experiment confirms that expectancy treatments can produce change.

There are a number of possible explanations for how expectancy manipulations produce change. One is that cognitive changes may have been produced which reduce anxiety. There is evidence that people can make themselves anxious by saying certain things to themselves. Often it is the anticipation and verbal rehearsal of an event which causes the most anxiety. Similarly, people may be able to reduce their fearfulness by reassuring themselves. For example, if after receiving a convincing therapy, a person were to say, "I am not afraid," the fear might be considerably reduced. Whether this mechanism in fact operates and accounts for much of the change produced by either expectancy manipulations or systematic desensitization is a matter of considerable controversy. At the present time there is much contradictory evidence with respect to the role of cognitive changes.

A second possible explanation is that expectancy manipulations produce improvement by motivating patients to expose themselves to phobic stimuli. After undergoing a "convincing therapy," patients may be more inclined to reality test, and this increased exposure could result in fear extinction and self-reinforcement for improvement. Thus, expectancy manipulations may be effective because of their inadvertent use of learning principles. (For a more complete discussion of these and other mechanisms, see Lick and Bootzin, in press.)

There are two strategies for investigating the role of expectancy in systematic desensitization. The first, as you have just read, is to devise expectancy manipulations which are as effective as systematic desensitization. If this could not have been done, a reasonable conclusion would have been that systematic desensitization involves processes other than expectancy. However, even though an effective placebo treatment was devised, it does not mean that systematic desensitization is an expectancy manipulation. There are still alternative hypotheses. For example, systematic desensitization and the expectancy manipulation could be equally effective for different reasons. Or alternatively, expectancy manipulations may be effective because of learning principles.

The second strategy for investigating the role of expectancy is more direct and involves inducing different expectations of outcome in the patients. This strategy is exemplified by a study by Donald Oliveau, W. Stewart Agras, Harold Leitenberg, Robert C. Moore, and Dale E. Wright (1969). One of the variables they investigated was the contribution of therapeutic instructions to the effectiveness of systematic desensitization with snake-fearful college women.[1]

In the Oliveau et al. study, all subjects were given systematic desensitization and told that they were participating in an experiment designed to gain "understanding of the relationship between certain physiological responses and the imagining of feared objects." Half the subjects were told that the method being used was therapeutic and had been successful in curing similar fears. Then they were told that they could expect their own fear of snakes to decrease. Thus, an expectancy for a positive outcome was induced. No mention of any therapeutic benefit was made to the remaining subjects. Instead, they were told that in order to provide an uncontaminated physiological record, they would be trained to reach a deep state of relaxation which would "eliminate extraneous factors."

To measure the degree of fear, subjects were tested before and after treatment as follows:

All Ss [subjects] were given a pre-test in which their fear of snakes was behaviorally measured on a scale ranging from 1 to 16. Formal testing was done in a room separate from that used for desensitization sessions. Instructions were programmed on a tape recorder such that each S received the same sequence of instructions with the same voice intonation. A 44 in. Holbrook (or Spotted) King snake was used. Ss were asked in a graded series of steps to approach the snake, to put their hand in the cage, and, finally, to pick up the snake. S was told in advance that she would be given instructions from a tape recorder but that she could stop at any point if she felt she was too afraid to attempt the next step [p. 28].

---

[1] Fear of snakes is often used as the target stimulus for such studies for two reasons. First, it is a frequently reported intense fear. This means that it is possible to recruit sufficient numbers of subjects to assign them randomly to different treatments. Second, the criteria for improvement can be specified (in this case, touching or holding a snake). Although fear of snakes is overrepresented in evaluation studies, all the techniques in this chapter have been applied successfully to more complicated problems as well.

After treatment the same procedure was repeated (but with a boa constrictor). The experimenter performing the pre- and posttests was given no information as to which instructions the subjects had received to ensure that he would not bias the results.

The results are illustrated in Figure 4-2. All subjects improved; however, those who received therapeutic instructions improved the most. From this study alone it is not clear whether the positive expectancy increased the effectiveness of systematic desensitization or whether the "neutral" expectancy decreased it. A more comprehensive study done by S. B. Miller (1972) clarifies this point. Miller included a group receiving no information at all in addition to groups receiving therapeutic and misleading instructions (i.e., instructions describing the procedures as an experiment in visualization).

The results indicated that systematic desensitization subjects receiving either therapeutic instructions or no information improved the same amount, and both of these groups improved more than subjects receiving systematic desensitization defined as an experiment in visualization. In a postexperimental interview, subjects receiving no information attributed therapeutic effectiveness to the procedure, while subjects receiving a mislead-

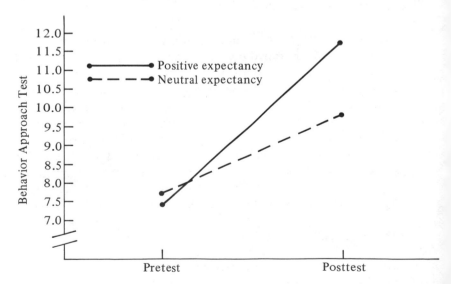

Figure 4-2
The effect of therapeutic instructions upon systematic desensitization. (Adapted from Oliveau et al., 1969.)

ing rationale *did not*. Apparently, misleading a subject about his participation affects both the subject's expectancy and the treatment outcome. This probably means that such subjects do not engage in the between-session behavior discussed earlier which would allow for increased exposure and self-reinforcement of improvement.

In a clinical setting, patients are not misled about their participation; they may be pessimistic or think that the treatment will not work, but they do know that they are receiving a "therapy." Thus, an important question is whether subjects will still improve if they are led to believe that systematic desensitization is ineffective. Marcia, Rubin, and Efran (1969) reported data which are relevant to this question. Half of the systematic desensitization subjects were told that they would be receiving "only the first *half* of treatment and that the treatment could not work without both halves." Surprisingly, this group of subjects improved just as much as the rest of the desensitization subjects. Later, when interviewed, it appeared that most of them had forgotten or ignored the expectancy manipulation. There are two possible interpretations of this finding. One is that the subjects had so much to remember that the expectancy manipulation was either not heard or easily forgotten. If this was the case, the negative expectancy was unsuccessfully induced and no information was provided as to whether subjects will improve when they do not expect to. The second interpretation is that since subjects were improving while receiving systematic desensitization, they forgot the instruction which was inconsistent with their improvement. In other words, since desensitization provides considerable feedback during the procedure itself, the evidence for improvement would have been more recent and more salient than the conflicting expectancy. Under these conditions, it is possible that the subject might discount the expectancy manipulation.

The second interpretation is supported by abundant anecdotal evidence from therapists that many subjects improve despite initial pessimism. The earlier example of Majid is a case in point. He was reluctant to seek a psychological treatment and quite skeptical of the likelihood of success. A more systematic assessment of what subjects expect was attempted by Albert Bandura and his colleagues (Bandura, Blanchard, and Ritter, 1969) as a part of a larger project evaluating systematic desensitization and other behavioral treatments. When snake-phobic subjects were first told about the type of treatment they would receive, 67 percent stated they did not expect to benefit. For example, one subject said:

> I felt totally unconfident that it would work on me. I thought I could probably get used to seeing snakes, but I never thought that I could be able to pick one up calmly. . . . I did not have much confidence in the method [p. 193].

Other subjects were disappointed that the treatment would be so symptom oriented; they expected a therapy that would explore the historical roots of the phobia:

> When I heard that it would be all involvement with snakes, I didn't think it would be successful in my case. I had expected and hoped for more discussion about snakes. However, I now realize that this would not have solved my problem. Rather, it would have been a waste of time [p. 194].

Irrespective of these negative and pessimistic expectancies, subjects did improve. Negative expectancies do not eliminate the effectiveness of systematic desensitization. In contrast, negative expectancies induced about placebo treatments do destroy their effectiveness (Marcia et al., 1969). Thus, unlike expectancy manipulations, systematic desensitization provides mechanisms for change despite skepticism and lack of enthusiasm.

The Therapeutic Computer

Peter Lang (1968) has explored the possibilities of having a computer give systematic desensitization to phobic subjects. First, the subject is interviewed by a therapist. During these sessions a hierarchy is constructed and the subject is given training in relaxation. Then the computer takes over. The computer, called DAD (Device for Automated Desensitization), is shown in Figure 4-3.

The subject sits in a comfortable chair listening to DAD through earphones. First, DAD administers relaxation instructions, and then it presents the initial item on the hierarchy. If the subject reports fear by pressing a switch in the left arm of the chair, the item is terminated and instructions to relax are given. Then the same item is presented again. DAD does not proceed to the next item until there have been two consecutive nonfearful presentations of an item.

If the subject signals fear to an item more than once, DAD asks whether the distress during the last presentation was worse than previously experienced. If the subject answers no, the item is repeated. A positive answer causes DAD to respond by moving back down the hierarchy one item to give the subject more practice with a less fearful item. In addition, DAD also records, for future use, the subject's physiological reactions (such as heart rate and galvanic skin response) throughout each session. The whole procedure can be repeated over a number of sessions until all items in the hierarchy have been covered.

The effectiveness of DAD with severely snake-phobic subjects has been evaluated by Peter Lang, Barbara Melamed, and James Hart (1970). Subjects were assigned to one of three groups: the DAD's automated desensitization, traditional desensitization with a therapist, and a no-treatment control group. Both the DAD and traditional desensitization subjects improved, whereas the no-treatment subjects did not. In addition, the DAD subjects showed just as much improvement as those receiving treatment from a therapist.

An obvious advantage of having a computer as an assistant is that it frees the therapist to handle more patients. The therapist does the initial interviewing, constructs the hierarchies, teaches the patient to relax, and then allows the computer to do the desensitization proper. While the computer is conducting the desensitization sessions, the therapist can be interviewing more patients. Another advantage (and this is the primary reason for developing such a system) is that more precise measurement of the patient's responses to the different elements of systematic desensitization is possible. Such parameters as the amount of time each scene should be visualized or the amount of relaxation to intersperse between scenes can be easily manipulated and their effects reliably measured (by means of both verbal reports and physiological data). The computer thus makes possible a more efficient investigation of the many complexities of systematic desensitization.

The fact that a computer can effectively carry out systematic desensitization has important theoretical implications. Successful computerized treatment means that it is unlikely that the relationship between therapist and patient is an essential component of the success of desensitization. Evidently, fear reduction can be ac-

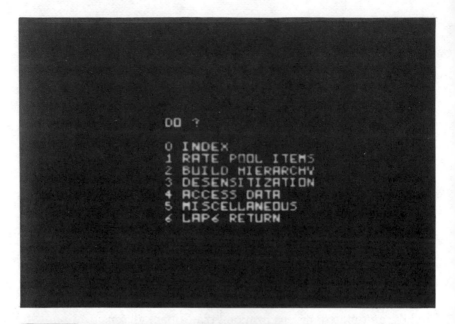

Figure 4-3
The desensitization program developed for the LINC-8 computer (DAD-1) performs several functions. Pools of fear items are available for specific phobias; they can be accessed from digital tape and presented to the subject for rating. The computer subsequently creates hierarchies from these ratings, according to instructions or rules concerning length and spacing. The desensitization procedure itself is also controlled by the computer. Fear items are presented in alpha-numeric

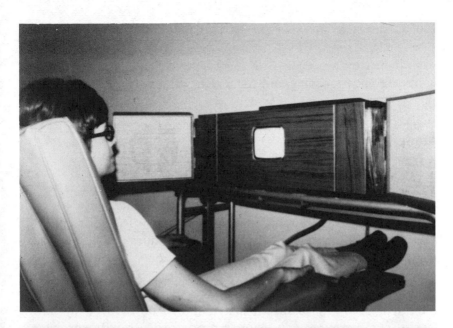

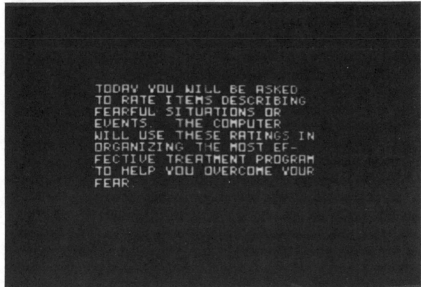

TODAY YOU WILL BE ASKED
TO RATE ITEMS DESCRIBING
FEARFUL SITUATIONS OR
EVENTS. THE COMPUTER
WILL USE THESE RATINGS IN
ORGANIZING THE MOST EF-
FECTIVE TREATMENT PROGRAM
TO HELP YOU OVERCOME YOUR
FEAR.

form on the oscilloscope. Relaxation and other instructions are presented from cartridge audio tapes. Feedback programs for physiological control are also available to the system.

At left, the experimenter-therapist is selecting a control function from the system tape. Above, the subject is looking at an instructional frame from the Pool Rating program. (Photos, courtesy Peter Lang.)

complished by a specified set of procedures and is not dependent upon the understanding and comfort of a therapist.

Modeling

The use of models of appropriate behavior as a technique for reducing fear has been evident in the psychological literature for some time. In fact, Mary Cover Jones, in her series of experiments with children in 1924, believed that of the techniques she tested modeling had the most potential—a potential only recently explored systematically.

Albert Bandura and his associates in a series of studies (see Bandura, 1971) have shown that fear can be reduced by having fearful subjects repeatedly observe models successfully engaging in the feared activities. This illustrates the principle of *vicarious extinction*. As Bandura has pointed out, repeated observations that feared performance does not lead to unfavorable consequences would be expected to extinguish both emotional responses and fear-arousing thoughts.

Even when using models, Bandura has found it beneficial to retain a graduated hierarchy; models perform a sequence of activities beginning with those which are the least feared. In one study (Bandura, Grusec, and Menlove, 1967) fear of dogs was reduced by having the children watch another child interact with a dog. The fear-eliciting quality of the interactions was increased gradually by controlling the physical restraints on the dog, and the intimacy and duration of the interactions.

Subsequent experiments have found that vicarious extinction is produced by filmed as well as live models. In addition, the effect of modeling was enhanced when multiple models were shown interacting with the feared object. The model's similarity to the subject might also be expected to enhance effectiveness. This has not been the case, however, for physical attributes such as age. Modeling is just as therapeutic when the model is clearly not the same age as the subject as it is when model and subject are peers (e.g., Bandura and Barab, 1973; Weissbrod and Bryan, 1973). A different dimension of similarity, the extent of fearfulness exhibited by the model, does produce differences in effectiveness.

Donald Meichenbaum (1971) found that coping models produced more fear reduction than mastery models. A coping model was one who started the task quite fearful and hesitant and only gradually became more confident in handling the "feared object" (in this case a snake). Mastery models, on the other hand, were confident throughout and "behaved as if the handling of snakes was commonplace." The effectiveness of the coping model was increased when the models verbalized reassuring statements to themselves as they engaged in the task. (Subjects were told that the students they were about to observe on videotape had been instructed to describe aloud what they were thinking during the assessment.) For example, one model said to the snake, "I'm going to make a deal with you; if you don't scare or hurt me, I won't scare or hurt you." Two subjects who had been exposed to the model offered the same deal to the snake during their own postassessment.

There are two explanations for the increased effectiveness of verbalizing coping models. One is that vicarious extinction was enhanced due to the increased similarity of the model to the subject. Another possibility (not incompatible with the first) is that the model taught the subject new strategies for coping with a stressful experience. The fact that some subjects repeated the models' sentences strengthens this interpretation.

Modeling thus provides the therapist with an opportunity to teach clients new cognitive strategies. In addition, the thoughts and feelings the client is likely to experience later can be included in the treatment. For example, a model for a treatment of nail-biting might say the following: "There I go again. Just this one nail, then I'll stop. . . . I knew the treatment wouldn't help me. I just can't control myself. Cut it out. You always make excuses for yourself. Take a slow, deep breath. Relax. Just think of myself sucking my finger in front of everyone. What a picture! . . ." (Meichenbaum, 1975).

As Meichenbaum (1975) has pointed out, this statement serves several purposes: it teaches cognitive and behavioral skills, it provides a model for success, and it alerts the client to self-defeating thoughts in which he might engage. But when such thoughts next occur, they will serve as reminders to carry out the newly acquired coping behaviors.

Modeling, with or without self-verbalization, can be an important component of many treatments for a variety of problems.

The next sections illustrate how modeling can be used in combination with other techniques.

MODELING PLUS GUIDED PARTICIPATION

A very successful variation of *in vivo* desensitization which combines modeling and guided participation is called *contact desensitization* and was developed by Brunhilde Ritter (1968). The therapist first *models* the appropriate behavior and then *guides* the subject through each step of the hierarchy. For example, if the subject were afraid of snakes, the following procedure would be used:

First, the therapist would model a variety of tasks, starting with approaching and touching the snake and continuing to more fearful items such as having the snake crawl loose around the therapist's shoulders. The subject would then be invited to perform the lowest task on the hierarchy with the therapist's aid. (The *contact* in contact desensitization refers to the contact between the therapist and patient, not the contact between the patient and the feared object.) Although a graded hierarchy is retained, relaxation training is not used. However, the patient repeats each item of the hierarchy until the anxiety associated with that item extinguishes.

Contact desensitization has been dramatically effective. In one study (Murphy and Bootzin, 1973), 93 percent of snake-fearful children were able to perform the terminal behavioral task after a maximum of only four eight-minute treatment sessions. Children who would not even touch a snake before treatment held it in their laps after treatment.

To assess whether all the elements in contact desensitization are essential, Brunhilde Ritter (1969) experimented with patients who were very fearful of heights. Subjects were given one of three treatments: modeling, modeling plus participation, and contact desensitization. All treatments took place on the roof of a seven-story building. A series of 44 height tasks was devised. The first task involved climbing a wooden ladder positioned in the center of the roof, next to a canopy which provided support for the subject during climbing. Each succeeding task involved less support and more exposure to the full seven-story height. Before treatment, subjects were able to complete about 7 of the 44 tasks.

Subjects receiving the modeling treatment observed the therapist performing each of the height tasks. Subjects in the modeling plus participation group observed the demonstration and were then asked to perform each of the steps that they could do comfortably. Subjects receiving contact desensitization observed the demonstration, were invited to perform each step, and received the assistance of the therapist who held the subject's arm or waist at various points in the procedure.

The results, after one 35-minute session, are presented in Figure 4-4. The contact desensitization group improved the most, followed next by the group receiving both modeling and participation. The least improvement accrued to the group which received only modeling.

Albert Bandura, Edward Blanchard, and Brunhilde Ritter (1969) compared contact and systematic desensitization. Snake-phobic patients received one of four treatments: contact desensitization, systematic desensitization, self-paced modeling, and a no-treatment control. The self-paced modeling treatment involved teaching subjects first to relax progressive relaxation. Then, subjects

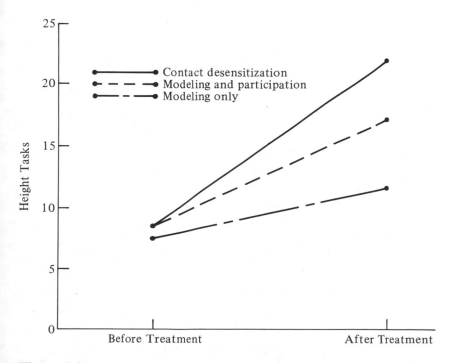

Figure 4-4
A comparison of modeling, modeling and participation, and contact desensitization. (From Ritter, 1969.)

viewed a film of a model performing a series of graduated tasks with snakes. However, in this case, the subjects were instructed to stop the film and replay a sequence whenever they felt anxious. They were to repeat this procedure until they could view the sequences while remaining completely relaxed. Thus, the procedure was similar to systematic desensitization except that the subject paced his own performance without the aid of the therapist and the stimuli were filmed rather than imagined.

Figure 4-5 shows the results of this experiment. The major criterion was a 28-step behavioral approach test. The contact desensitization group improved remarkably. In fact, 11 of the 12 subjects performed the final item on the approach test. Symbolic modeling and systematic desensitization produced improvement but were not as effective as contact desensitization.

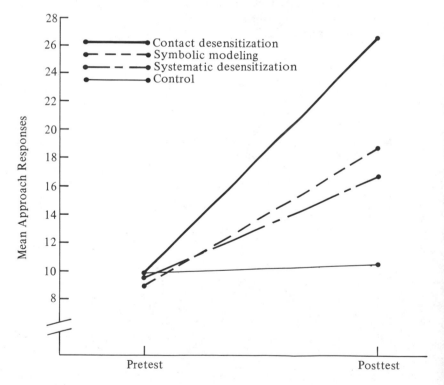

Figure 4-5
Mean number of approach responses performed by subjects before and after receiving their respective treatments. (Adapted from Bandura, Blanchard, and Ritter, 1969.)

A very important component of contact desensitization is that it involves actual contact with the feared stimulus. This component probably accounts for its superiority to symbolic modeling and systematic desensitization in the above evaluation. It should be noted that in the clinical use of systematic desensitization, this component is incorporated into the treatment by requiring patients to test out their improvement in real-life situations. This increased exposure is likely to result in additional fear extinction.

Behavior Rehearsal

In contact desensitization the patient actively performs nonfearful behavior; in a sense, the patient practices being fearless. This principle has been applied to assertive behavior as well. A person who is inhibited, unassertive, or socially inept can also practice until he or she performs assertive responses comfortably and without anxiety. This procedure has been called *behavior rehearsal*. It usually involves modeling, instruction, and repeated practice.

ASSERTIVE BEHAVIOR

Andrew Salter (1949) was one of the earliest researchers to suggest procedures for the teaching of assertive behavior. He developed six rules that clients were to practice. They are: (1) Verbally express your feelings; that is, let people know when you are happy, sad, determined, angry, and so forth. (2) Show your emotions nonverbally. If you are happy, smile and look happy; if angry, scowl. (3) When you disagree with someone, contradict them. Do not sit quietly. (4) Use the pronoun *I* as much as possible. (5) Express agreement when praised. (6) Improvise; live for the moment.

Many of Salter's suggestions have worn well with time and have been incorporated in more systematic attempts to teach assertive behavior. Salter relied primarily upon persuasion to induce clients to act more assertively. Later treatments have relied more upon modeling, instruction, and repeated practice.

The following case study treated by Arnold Lazarus (Wolpe and Lazarus, 1966) gives a feeling for the complexity of the task.

Problems in both verbal and nonverbal behavior have to be identified and altered. The client (P. R.) was a 39-year-old man who, although highly qualified for an executive position, had not achieved one. He attributed his junior status to his inability to act assertively. In order to advance, he felt that he had to seek different employment but was terrified at the prospect of being interviewed. So employment interviews were made the focus for his behavior rehearsal.

> Mr. P. R. was told to pretend that the therapist was a prominent business executive who had advertised for an experienced accountant to take charge of one of his companies. Mr. P. R. had applied for the position and had been asked to present himself for an interview. The therapist instructed Mr. P. R. to leave the consulting room, to knock on the door and to enter when invited to do so (see below).
>
> At the therapist's deliberately resonant "Come in!" Mr. P. R. opened the door of the consulting room and hesitantly approached the desk. The therapist interrupted the role-playing procedure to mirror the patient's timid posture, shuffling gait, downcast eyes and overall tension. Mr. P. R. was required to sit at the desk and to play the role of the prominent business executive while the therapist reenacted Mr. P. R.'s entry into the room. The patient was asked to criticize the therapist's performance. The therapist then modeled the entry of an "assertive individual," asking the patient to note the impact of variations in posture and gait and the all-important absence or presence of eye-contact.
>
> The "correct" entry was rehearsed several times until Mr. P. R.'s approach to the prominent-executive-behind-the-desk was completely devoid of any overt signs of timidity or anxiety. He was then taught to deal with a variety of entries—being met at the door; the employer who makes himself incommunicado while studying important looking documents; and the overeffusive one who self-consciously tries to place him at ease.
>
> Next, the content of the interview was scrutinized. Mr. P. R.'s replies to questions concerning his background, qualifications and experience were tape-recorded. Mr. P. R. was instructed to place himself in the position of the prospective employer and asked to decide whether or not he would employ the applicant on the basis of his recorded interview. It was clear from the recording that the elimination of Mr. P. R.'s hesitant gait and posture had not generalized to his faltering speech. Above all, it was noted Mr. P. R.

tended to undersell himself. Instead of stressing his excellent qualifications he mumbled rather incoherent and unimpressive generalities about his background and training. The therapist demonstrated more efficient verbal responses which the patient was required to imitate. In this manner, Mr. P. R. was able to rehearse adequate replies to specific questions, and to prepare an impressive-sounding discourse for use in unstructured interviews.

The above-mentioned procedures were employed during five therapeutic sessions held at weekly intervals. Mr. P. R. cancelled his sixth appointment and did not communicate for approximately 2 months. He then made another appointment. On entering the consulting room, he said, "You are looking at the Chief Accountant of . . ." (a very large industrial organization). He then described how he had replied to the advertisement, been exposed to three separate interviews ("You would have been proud of your handiwork . . . I handled them with such aplomb!") and how he was finally offered the post at an even higher salary than advertised.

Mr. P. R. proclaimed himself "cured." Although the therapist felt that many remaining facets of Mr. P. R.'s interpersonal dealings warranted additional assertive training, he did not discourage him from terminating therapy (on the understanding that he was free to resume should he deem it necessary).

Five years later Mr. P. R. telephoned the therapist to report that he had become principal economic advisor to an important mining concern [pp. 49–50].

An experimental demonstration of the effectiveness of behavior rehearsal was performed by Richard McFall and Albert Marston (1970) with nonassertive college students. Subjects were assigned to either behavior rehearsal, placebo therapy control, or no-treatment control.

Subjects assigned to behavior rehearsal received four sessions of treatment. During each session the subject listened to tape recordings of dialogue covering six situations. When a bell sounded, the subject was told to respond to the dialogue in as appropriately assertive a manner as possible.

The following is the transcript of a typical training stimulus (McFall and Marston, 1970):

Narrator: Imagine that this morning you took your car to a local Standard Station, and you explicitly told the mechanic to give you a simple tune-up. The bill should have been $20. It's now later in the afternoon and you're at the station to pick up your car. The mechanic is walking over to you.

Mechanic: "Okay, let me make out a ticket for you. The tune-up was $12 for parts and $8 for labor. Oh, grease and oil job was $6. Anti-freeze was $5. Uh, $4 for a new oil filter. And, uh, $5 for rotating the tires. That's $40 in all. Will this be cash or charge?"

In the first training session, a bell would sound at this point as a cue for the subject to respond.

The subject would practice this scene four times before starting the next scene. During the second session, the same six scenes would be presented again. This time, however, the subject would not be asked to respond until later in the script. This way the subject would be required to respond to a directly hostile antagonist for two trials and an indirectly hostile one for the remaining two trials.

The following is the continuation of the gas station transcript. The subject hears the tape from the beginning, but instead of responding, hears:

Narrator: You say to him, "What? I told you just to give it a tune-up. I don't feel I should have to pay for all those extras, unless you can convince me that they are necessary!"

Then on two trials:

Mechanic: (Gruff, irritated) "Look, you brought your car in here to have it fixed. I fixed it! Now, will this be cash or charge?" [Bell. Subject responds.]

On the other two trials:

Mechanic: (Holier than thou) "I realize that you only wanted a tune-up, but we base our reputation on quality service and customer satisfaction, so we made the extra repairs because we felt they were necessary to keep you satisfied." [Bell. Subject responds.]

During sessions three and four, subjects practiced six new situations. In total, subjects had eight rehearsals of each of 12 situations.

The placebo therapy subjects also met for four sessions. The subjects discussed their inability to be assertive and were encouraged by their therapists to be more assertive. If and when subjects reported attempts to be assertive, the therapist verbally reinforced them. Thus, the "placebo" was fairly typical verbal counseling.

To assess improvement a number of measures were administered before and after treatment. The primary measure was having the subjects respond to tape-recorded dialogue depicting 16 situations, all of which were different from those used during therapy. Subjects receiving behavior rehearsal showed more improvement than subjects in the placebo and no-treatment control groups.

To test whether the treatment generalized outside the laboratory, every subject was phoned by a "magazine salesman" two weeks after treatment. Subjects who received behavior rehearsal took less time to show resistance to the salesman than those in the other groups.

Richard McFall and Craig Twentyman (1973) in a series of studies have further investigated behavior rehearsal by evaluating the contributions of coaching, different types of models (tactful or abrupt), and different types of practice (out loud or silent). Their findings have been that coaching and either type of practice helped produce improvement, whereas modeling the responses contributed little to the effectiveness of the treatment.

Another group of researchers (Hersen, Eisler, and Miller, 1974) has investigated assertive training, but with hospitalized psychiatric patients instead of college students. Patients received practice on five scenes and were evaluated on the five they practiced and an additional five. When modeling was part of the treatment, the subject watched a videotape of a model responding to the training scene. For the evaluation, the patients' responses to a research assistant were videotaped and rated for components of assertiveness such as eye contact, loudness of voice, and overall assertiveness.

Patients receiving a combined treatment of modeling, instruction, and practice were more assertive on all scenes than were patients who only practiced the responses. An earlier study (Hersen et al., 1973) found that the combined treatment was more effective than treatments that omitted either modeling or instructions.

These were analog rather than treatment studies, even though psychiatric patients were evaluated. The patients were recruited for research, not for treatment. An important question is the extent to which this training would generalize to situations outside of the lab. Hersen, Eisler, and Miller (1974) attempted to assess this by giving each patient only $1.00 in canteen booklets for his participation instead of the promised $3.00 in booklets. The patients' responses were videotaped and rated. (The research assistant stopped patients who did not object to being short-changed before they left and corrected the "error.") Unfortunately, there was no difference between groups on amount of assertiveness exhibited in this situation. Patients in all groups were moderately assertive.

Controlled studies of assertive training have not yet captured the richness of the procedures illustrated by the Lazarus case study. Treatments have not been individualized and insufficient attention has been paid to identifying the areas of functioning for which assertive training would be required.

Attentiveness and Other Behaviors

Behavior rehearsal is used not only as a treatment for unassertiveness; it can be used to help teach any number of responses. One particularly interesting use has been suggested by Donald Meichenbaum and Roy Cameron (1973). They used behavior rehearsal to teach schizophrenics self-instructional statements as a means of controlling inattentiveness.

The patients were taught how to deal with interviews and intelligence subtests. The experimenter first modeled the appropriate performance and self-statements, using a coping rather than mastery style, and then instructed the patient; then the patient practiced the same task, initially speaking self-instructions aloud and later covertly. On complex tasks, the patients were taught to monitor and evaluate their behavior by means of self-questioning.

The following is an example of one of the experimenter-modeled self-statements for answering a question asking in what way two objects are alike.

I have to figure out how a fly and a tree are alike. A fly and a tree? (pause). A fly is small and a tree is big. I got it, the fly can carry germs to the tree . . . (pause). No, that doesn't make sense. That doesn't tell me how they are alike. I have to see how they are alike. Go slowly and think this one out. Don't just say the first thing that comes to mind. (Pause while the model thinks.) I want to give the best answer I can. Let me imagine in my mind the objects . . . fly, tree . . . out in the sunshine. They both need sunshine to live. That is it, they are both living things. Good, I figured it out. If I take my time and just think about how the two objects are alike, I can do it [Meichenbaum and Cameron, 1973].

For interviews, patients were taught self-statements such as "It's not clear, let me try again" and "Give healthy talk, be coherent."

Five patients received the complete training program, while another five patients practiced the same items without modeling or instruction. On four of five posttest measures the self-instructed patients performed much better than the practice controls (on the fifth there was no difference between the groups). Most importantly, the percentage of "sick-talk" (judges rated the patients' answers as to their relevance and coherence) in response to interview questions decreased from about 60 percent to less than 20 percent for schizophrenics who received self-instruction training. This improvement was maintained in a follow-up series of assessments taken three weeks later. This study is an important demonstration that it is possible to teach schizophrenics to function more effectively using modeling and behavior rehearsal.

Flooding and Implosive Therapy

The treatments described so far in this chapter are all structured to minimize anxiety arousal. In contrast, flooding is rapid *in vivo* exposure to anxiety-eliciting stimuli with no attempt to minimize arousal. It would be expected that repeated exposure would lead to fear extinction.

Flooding (often preceded by modeling) has been used effectively as a treatment for obsessive-compulsive rituals (e.g., Rachman, Marks, and Hodgson, 1973). Such rituals generally fall into one of two categories: contamination fears with washing rituals and repetitive checking rituals. Flooding for contamination fears involves inducing patients to contaminate themselves and then preventing them from carrying out the rituals. Patients with checking compulsions are similarly induced to engage in activities they have avoided and are also prevented from carrying out their rituals.

For example, one patient avoided any activity which might conceivably bring harm to someone. His obsessional thoughts could only be terminated by constantly checking to make sure that he completed some activity correctly. He checked to make sure that water was not running, razor blades were put away, mats were not ruffled, and so on.

Treatment involved having him drive a car, bump into people in a supermarket, put pins, matches, and a stone on the floor, and turn on faucets and leave them dripping. The therapist modeled the behavior first and then instructed the patient to perform it. The patient was also instructed to resist the urge to check, and he was not allowed to ask whether harm to anyone resulted from his actions (Hodgson, Rachman, and Marks, 1972).

S. Rachman, I. Marks, and R. Hodgson (1973) evaluated flooding, modeling, and flooding plus modeling in comparison to relaxation treatment. Relaxation was ineffective in altering obsessive-compulsive rituals. On the other hand, after only three weeks of treatment all three of the exposure treatments were quite effective, and improvement was maintained at a six-month follow-up. Although there was little difference in effectiveness among the three exposure treatments, Rachman and his colleagues recommended that the combined flooding and modeling treatment be used until further research demonstrated the superiority of one component over the other.

IMPLOSIVE THERAPY

Implosive therapy is a variation of flooding in which the anxiety-eliciting stimuli are thoughts and images. Thomas Stampfl, who created implosive therapy, reasoned that if anxiety is a conditioned response (CR), images and thoughts about dreaded events would be conditioned stimuli (CS). The unconditioned stimulus (UCS) is the real pain which would be experienced if the dreaded event occurred. Thus, if the CS were presented repeatedly in the absence of the UCS, extinction would occur. However, since ordinarily the patient avoids the CS (tries not to think about things of which he is afraid), it is never extinguished.

For example, the CS for a patient afraid of snakes is the

images and thoughts about snakes; the CR is the fear elicited by the thoughts; and the UCS is the pain associated with being bitten by a snake. If the patient thinks about snakes (the CS), he becomes anxious (the CR); but if the patient is not actually bitten (the UCS), the anxiety associated with thinking about snakes should be extinguished. Since the patient avoids thinking about snakes (to avoid the anxiety), the procedure in implosive therapy is to force the patient to think about them. The goal of the therapy, then, is to extinguish the anxiety associated with thoughts about feared events. A successfully treated patient would still exercise caution around poisonous snakes but would not be fearful (see Stampfl and Levis, 1967).

A type of hierarchy of scenes is employed in implosive therapy. Whereas the hierarchy in desensitization is used to minimize the amount of anxiety experienced, the hierarchy in implosive therapy is intended to prolong the anxiety. The therapist escalates the scenes to keep the patient anxious as long as possible. Eventually, the anxiety associated with such scenes is extinguished and the therapist is unable to elicit anxiety by describing them.

The following excerpts are taken from a case reported by Robert Hogan (1968) in which implosive therapy was used to treat snake phobia. After having the patient imagine holding a snake, the therapist escalates the scenes:

Okay, now put your finger out towards the snake and feel his head coming up. . . . It heads towards your finger and it is starting to bite at your finger. Let it, let it bite at your finger. Put your finger out, let it bite, let it bite at your finger, feel its fangs go right down into your finger. Oooh, feel the pain going right up your arm and into your shoulder. You want to pull your hand away, but leave it there. Let the snake kind of gnaw at your finger. Feel it gnawing, look at the blood dripping off your finger. Feel it in your stomach and the pain going up your arm. . . .

Okay, feel him coiling around your hand again, touching you, slimy, now he is going up your shoulder and he crawls there and he is sitting on your chest and he is looking you right in the eye. He is big and he is black and he is ugly and he's coiled up and he is ready to strike and he is looking at you. Picture his face. Look at his eyes. Look at those long sharp fangs. . . . Feel him bite at your face. . . . Let him bite at your face; feel his fangs go right into your cheeks; and the blood is coming out on your face now. And the poison is going into your body and you are getting sick and nauseated and he is striking at your face again and again. . . . Picture what your face looks like. Get that sick feeling in your stomach and now he is gnawing at your nose, and biting at your mouth. Just take a deep breath and let him do it.

The therapist continues to escalate the scenes:

It is kind of gnawing on it and eating, eating at your eye. Your little eye is down on your cheek and it is gnawing and biting at your eye. Picture it. Now it is crawling into your eye socket and wiggling around in there, feel it wiggling and wiggling up in your head. Feel it wiggling around, uhhh uhhh, feel it wiggling. And now it wiggles out of your eye, and now it is wiggling up into your nose. Feel it crawling right up into your nose, into your head, wiggling around and it is gnawing out through the other eye, from the inside. Feel it biting its way out [Hogan, 1968, pp. 427–28].

The therapist continues to elaborate and expand such scenes, session after session, until the patient can no longer become anxious in response to such scenes.

Although implosive therapy has not been investigated as thoroughly as systematic desensitization, there have been some experiments evaluating its effectiveness. Curtis Barrett (1969) compared the effects of implosive therapy, systematic desensitization, and a no-treatment control group on adults who were afraid of harmless snakes. Barrett found that both systematic desensitization and implosive therapy resulted in dramatic improvement in a behavioral approach test administered at the end of treatment. Before treatment started, the average subject was unable to come closer than five feet to the snake. At the end of treatment, 11 of 12 subjects receiving systematic desensitization and 10 of 12 subjects receiving implosive therapy were able to at least touch the snake. Six months later, the subjects receiving systematic desensitization had maintained their gains, but a few implosive therapy patients had relapsed. Although implosive therapy was generally effective, improvement was not as consistent as it was with systematic desensitization.

Barrett also reported some unpleasant between-session reactions of subjects receiving implosive therapy. For example, one subject began to imagine snakes every time she closed her eyes.

This interfered with sleeping and other aspects of her life. She was very reluctant to continue the therapy; however, after being persuaded to continue, she did improve. She was able to hold the snake at the posttest and six months later; and, after therapy, thoughts of snakes no longer intruded whenever she closed her eyes.

Even though implosive therapy is often very effective, the more consistent effects of systematic desensitization and the decreased danger of untoward reactions during treatment make systematic desensitization the preferred treatment for reducing anxiety.

Systematic Habituation

Techniques which combine increased exposure with a graduated hierarchy have also been suggested (Bootzin and Kazdin, 1972; D'Zurilla, Wilson, and Nelson, 1973). Bootzin and Kazdin called their procedure *systematic habituation* and compared its effectiveness to systematic desensitization with 27 height-fearful subjects solicited through newspaper stories.

Subjects receiving systematic habituation were taught to relax and constructed a hierarchy of fear-eliciting scenes. During the presentation of scenes, however, the subject was required to continue imagining a scene until he habituated to it—i.e., until the scene no longer elicited anxiety. (This is in contrast to systematic desensitization, in which the patient is instructed to stop imagining the scene at the first indication of anxiety.) If after five minutes the subject was still signaling anxiety, the scene was terminated, additional relaxation instructions were given, and the same scene was readministered. The item would be repeatedly presented in this manner until it no longer elicited anxiety, at which point the next scene in the hierarchy would be presented.

The results indicated that systematic desensitization and systematic habituation were equally efficient—each requiring an average of about eight sessions to finish the subject's hierarchy—and equally effective—demonstrating more improvement than the no-treatment control group on a variety of measures. This improvement was maintained at a six-month follow-up.

An advantage of systematic habituation over implosive therapy is that by retaining a graduated hierarchy, between-session disturbances should be minimized. One subject, however, did report an increase in nightmares related to her fear of heights as the end of the hierarchy was approached in treatment. This particular subject had a previous history of nightmares. To be on the safe side, this subject was switched from systematic habituation to systematic desensitization, continuing from the point of her last successfully passed item. Nightmares disappeared and the subject completed the hierarchy. At the end of treatment she was so delighted with her progress that she took her therapist out to dinner at the top of the John Hancock building in Chicago.

Thus, it appears possible to alternate between systematic desensitization and habituation without adverse effect, although future research will be required to evaluate whether such combinations of treatment are more effective than either treatment alone. One possible advantage of being able to alternate between treatments is that the therapy can be paced to the progress of the subject. For some subjects it may be helpful to use habituation within the framework of desensitization to get beyond items causing particular difficulty and, alternately, one could switch to desensitization from habituation if the treatment became too stressful.

Systematic desensitization is of proven effectiveness for reducing anxiety. Additional research on variations such as systematic habituation will be necessary before desensitization is replaced as the treatment of choice.

Recommended Readings

Bandura, A. Psychotherapy based upon modeling principles. In A. Bergin & S. Garfield (Eds.), *Handbook of psychotherapy and behavior change*. New York: Wiley, 1971.

Paul, G. L. Outcome of systematic desensitization: I. Background procedures, and uncontrolled reports of individual treatment. In C. M. Franks (Ed.), *Behavior therapy: Appraisal and status*. New York: McGraw-Hill, 1969.

Paul, G. L. Outcome of systematic desensitization: II. Controlled investigations of individual treatment, technique variations, and current status. In C. M. Franks (Ed.), *Behavior therapy: Appraisal and status*. New York: McGraw-Hill, 1969.

5

Punishment and Aversive Conditioning

In this chapter we will discuss techniques employing aversive stimuli. In accordance with the distinction made in Chapter 4, such techniques can be divided into operant and classical conditioning procedures. The first half of the chapter will focus on punishment (the operant techniques), and the second half will focus on aversive conditioning (the classical conditioning techniques).

Punishment

A major argument against the use of punishment as a behavior change technique has been that it only temporarily suppresses behavior. However, evidence from animal laboratories has indicated that punishment can be very effective (for excellent reviews of this material see Solomon, 1964, and Azrin and Holz, 1966).

Self-destructiveness. With human subjects, one of the most dramatic demonstrations of the effectiveness of punishment has come from Lovaas's work with self-destructive psychotic children. These children engage in a variety of self-injurious acts including hitting themselves in the face and banging their heads against the wall. The children may inflict such severe damage to themselves if left unattended that nursing personnel may feel compelled to keep them in restraints.

117

Because someone is likely to intervene and rescue a child from self-injury, it has been hypothesized that such personal attention may be reinforcing the self-destructiveness. This analysis would suggest that self-injurious acts could be extinguished if no one responded to them. Obviously this is a poor strategy if children are likely to cause serious damage to themselves before the response is extinguished.

The question remains, however, whether extinction would be a feasible strategy for self-destructive children who are less likely to hurt themselves seriously. Data on this question have been reported by Bradley Bucher and O. Ivar Lovaas (1968). One of the children they worked with was a 7-year-old retarded boy (IQ 25) named John, whom the staff considered a "careful hitter."

John had been self-destructive since the age of two and was hospitalized at the age of six. During his year in the hospital, he was kept in restraints 24 hours a day. Whenever the restraints were removed, he would "hit his head against the crib, beat his head with his fists, and scream."

To extinguish John's self-injurious acts, he was left alone in bed, without restraints, for an hour and a half each day. No attention was given to self-destructiveness. Figure 5-1 presents the record of the frequency with which John hit himself during each session. During the first session, John hit himself approximately three thousand times. By the eighth session, however, he only hit himself 15 times during the hour and a half. Although John obviously had improved, he had hit himself over ten thousand times in the process. Clearly, extinction is too prolonged and dangerous a procedure to use with most self-destructive children.

Neither extinction nor keeping the child in restraints seems to be a viable method of dealing with self-destructiveness, yet something must be done to suppress such behavior. To meet this dilemma, Lovaas and his colleagues explored the use of punishment. For some children, a loud "no" was sufficient to suppress some behaviors; for other children "a painful slap on the child's buttocks" worked. However, if these methods failed and alternate interventions were ruled out, electric shock was used as the punishing stimulus. Although not dangerous to the child, it was very painful.

One case reported by Bucher and Lovaas (1968) was of a 7½-year-old girl named Linda. She was diagnosed as retarded (IQ 33) and was so severely self-destructive that it had been necessary to

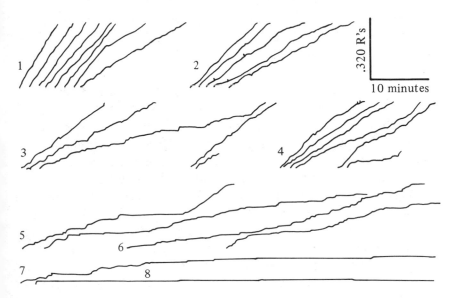

Figure 5-1
John's self-destructive behavior in the bed, in cumulative response curves, as a function of successive extinction sessions (labeled 1 through 8). (From Bucher and Lovaas, 1968.)

keep her in restraints throughout her entire period of hospitalization (1½ years). She was allowed to move around the ward only if her hands were tied to her thighs. If the restraints were removed, she immediately began to hit herself about her head and ears.

Two experimental sessions a day were scheduled during which she was allowed to walk around the ward without restraints. During baseline sessions (before any punishment was tried) she engaged in an average of about two hundred self-injurious acts per session. After the baseline sessions, Linda was shocked each time she began to hit herself. Immediately, her self-destructiveness dropped dramatically. After only four sessions and a total of only 15 shocks, Linda no longer was self-destructive. Even after shock no longer was administered, the frequency of her self-injurious acts remained at zero.

Although self-destructiveness was effectively suppressed, it is reasonable to be concerned about the possibility of detrimental side effects. Bucher and Lovaas also were concerned about this possibility and recorded the number of times Linda cried and avoided adults. Linda engaged in both of these acts at a very high frequency before treatment. Concurrent with the suppression of self-injurious behavior, Linda both decreased her crying and avoided adults less. Apparently the use of punishment, here, had beneficial side effects. An additional bonus, of course, was that once the staff no longer had to hover over the child to prevent her from hurting herself, a treatment program directed at her deficits could be started.

Since children who hit themselves probably are experiencing considerable pain, it seems paradoxical that the pain associated with shock would stop self-destructive behavior. One possible explanation for this may be that the child increased his or her tolerance for *self-induced* pain gradually. Electric shock, in contrast, is administered from the beginning of treatment at a very painful intensity. In fact, a sure way to have such a treatment program fail would be to start with very low levels of shock and then gradually increase the intensity. Under such circumstances, the child most certainly would learn to tolerate the pain and the undesirable behavior would not be suppressed.

Obviously, painful shock should be employed only if other more humane procedures are not effective. However, if the choice is to be between 15 painful shocks and years of being tied in restraints, it hardly can be argued that choosing to administer shock is the less humane choice.

Chronic ruminative vomiting. Another dramatic example of the use of shock as punishment has been reported by Peter Lang and Barbara Melamed (1969). They reported the treatment of a nine-month-old male infant whose life was endangered because he vomited all his food. He first had started vomiting when he was five months old. The problem continued to worsen until he was vomiting after every meal. No organic cause for the vomiting was discovered, even though he was hospitalized three times briefly for medical examinations.

At nine months of age he was admitted for his fourth hospitalization. The hospital staff tried several therapies without success. These included dietary changes, drugs, feeding the infant in different positions, giving him small amounts of food, and burping him frequently. Because thumbsucking usually accompanied vomiting, he was placed in restraints—also without effect. Intensive nursing care was given " 'to establish and maintain a one-to-one relationship and to provide the child with warm, friendly, and secure feelings' " (p. 3). This was abandoned because it did not decrease the frequency of vomiting and instead seemed to make the child uncomfortable.

By the time Lang and Melamed were consulted, the child's weight had dropped from 17 pounds at six months of age to 12 pounds at nine months of age (Figure 5-2A). Since all other methods had failed and the child's life was considered endangered if the vomiting could not be stopped, a punishment procedure was tried.

First, two days were spent observing the infant during and after meals. In addition, the muscle activity of the throat was measured by means of an electromyograph (EMG). This made it possible to note physiologically the first signs of vomiting.

The treatment consisted of a combination of punishment (using electric shock) and negative reinforcement. As soon as muscle activity in the throat indicated the beginning of vomiting, the child was shocked on the leg. EMG activity was particularly useful in helping the therapists confirm that only muscle activity associated with vomiting and not with other activities (such as sucking) was punished. The shock pulses (1-second shock and 1-second interval) continued until vomiting stopped. In this way, starting to vomit was punished (by the onset of shock) and inhibiting the vomit was negatively reinforced (by the termination of shock). Treatment sessions were given once a day for an hour beginning after a meal.

By the third session, the child was successful in inhibiting his vomiting and was rarely shocked. By the sixth session, the child was no longer vomiting during the treatment sessions. After three successive vomit-free sessions, the treatment was discontinued. Two days later, the child vomited again and three more treatment sessions were given to ensure that the problem behavior was completely suppressed. Five days after the last of these sessions, the child was discharged and already had begun to gain weight, weighing 16 pounds at discharge (see Figure 5-2B). Five months later, follow-up information indicated that vomiting had not reoccurred and that the child had gained an additional 10 pounds (see Figure 5-2C).

Other therapists who have treated ruminating infants have sometimes been effective by using punishing stimuli other than shock. For example, Thomas Sajwaj, Julian Libet, and Stewart Agras (1974) devised a treatment in which lemon juice was squirted into the mouth of the infant when she started to ruminate. However, the

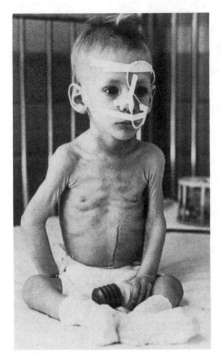

Figure 5-2
(A) Prior to treatment, the patient is clearly debilitated, with a lack of body fat and skin hanging in loose folds. The tape around the face holds tubing for the naso-gastric pump. (B) At hospital discharge, 13 days later, the patient has already attained a 26 percent increase in body weight. (C) shows the patient five months after treatment. (From Lang and Melamed, 1969.)

A

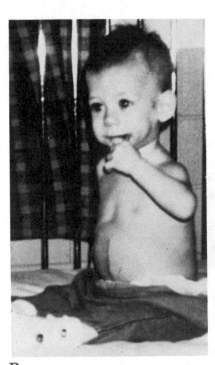

B

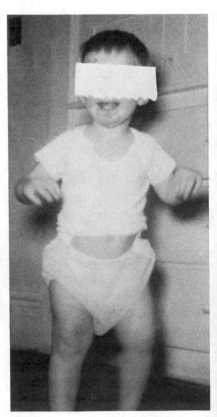

C

treatment took eight weeks, during which time the child remained hospitalized. Shock worked more rapidly, and the Lang and Melamed infant required only two weeks of hospitalization. In life-threatening situations, the speed with which the treatment is effective may be crucial.

In these cases, as in others previously mentioned, a treatment applied specifically to a problem behavior was dramatically successful even though no direct information about the cause of the problem was available. Frequently we can only speculate about the cause even when we know how to change the behavior. In the Lang and Melamed case there was considerable family stress which *might* have contributed to the development of the problem. The child's mother broke her ankle, which forced the family to move in with the maternal grandparents for several weeks. It was during this period of time that the vomiting started. There were several arguments between the child's mother and her own adoptive mother about the care of the child. In addition to that, a social worker's report suggested that the parents were making only a marginal marital adjustment. Although it is conceivable that stresses in the family contributed to the child's problem, therapies generated by such an orientation (such as developing a strong one-to-one relationship with the child) were not successful.

As we have discussed in relation to other therapies, "No evidence of 'symptom substitution' was observed following treatment. On the other hand, positive social behavior increased coincident with the successful conditioning therapy. The infant became more responsive to adults, smiled more frequently, and seemed to be more interested in toys and games than he had been previously" (Lang and Melamed, 1969, p. 7).

OVERCORRECTION

Electric shock is not the only effective punishment. Nathan Azrin and his colleagues have developed a procedure which they call *overcorrection*. The underlying principle is that a disruptive response will decrease in frequency if the offender is required to overcorrect by restoring the environment to better than its original condition. These techniques have been applied primarily with institutionalized retardates but would be more generally applicable as well.

Foxx and Azrin (1972) described how overcorrection could

be used in eliminating aggressive behavior. A retarded 50-year-old woman (IQ 16) was a major problem on her ward because she was constantly throwing and overturning beds, chairs, and tables. She had been doing this for over 35 years. A number of techniques to eliminate this behavior had been tried by the staff without success. These included physical restraint, seclusion, and requiring her to restore the overturned furniture to its original place.

The overcorrection procedure specified that she receive "Household Orderliness" training and "Social Reassurance" training for a minimum of 30 minutes for each incident. Household Orderliness training meant that the patient had to put all furniture back into its correct position *and* spend the rest of the 30 minutes straightening other furniture and dusting and cleaning the rest of the ward. If beds were overturned, she was required to remake the beds she overturned and then smooth out and straighten other beds on the ward. Social Reassurance training meant that the patient had to apologize to all people whose beds or chairs had been thrown and to all other people on the ward who might have been frightened by her actions. Although she could hardly speak, she could nod her head in answer to questions about whether she was sorry about the disturbance and whether she intended to do it again.

Before these procedures were instituted, the patient threw about 13 objects a day. After two weeks of the contingent application of overcorrection she averaged fewer than 1 object a day. The procedures were continued until by the eleventh week she had stopped throwing objects entirely—and this was accomplished in spite of a 35-year history with this problem.

RESPONSE COST

Other punishment procedures, such as response cost, are commonly used to control behavior in our society but have been applied systematically by behavior therapists only in the past few years. One demonstration was reported by Alan Kazdin (1971) with a 29-year-old retarded woman (IQ 42) who worked in a sheltered workshop. She had a long-standing problem of blurting out startling statements while working. This had led to her being diagnosed as "prepsychotic." "While some of her statements were ostensibly meaningful, others were considered in prior psychiatric evaluations to reveal hallucinations or ideas of reference (i.e., 'My name is Lady Mary [a fictitious character]' or 'You can't take that away from me')" (Kazdin, 1971).

Baseline data collected for four weeks showed that she blurted out statements over 40 times a day. Each morning of the fifth week the client was told that she would lose one token whenever she blurted out (a token economy had previously been set up in the workshop). In fact, the consequence was not carried out during this week. As can be seen in Figure 5-3, *threatening* to take away tokens had no effect on the frequency of her vocalizations. For the following three weeks, she actually was fined one token per vocalization. There was an immediate and dramatic effect. Increasing the fine to two tokens suppressed the frequency even more. Even after the

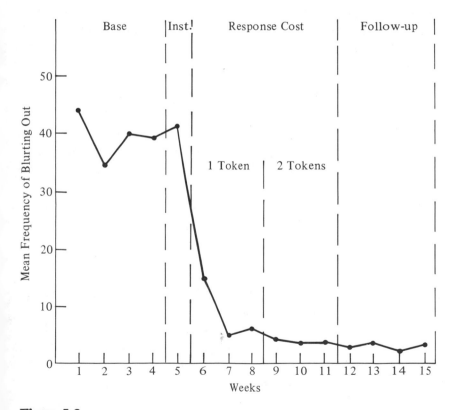

Figure 5-3
Average frequency of inappropriate vocalizations. (From Kazdin, 1971.)

negative punishment procedures were terminated, the frequency of vocalizations stayed very low (an average of 1.2 times per day).

An important implication of these results was the ease with which a "psychotic symptom" was altered. In fact, since her verbalizations were the only evidence of "prepsychotic behavior," without them it is unlikely that the client would receive the same diagnosis.

Time-out from positive reinforcement. Another commonly used response cost procedure is *time-out from positive reinforcement*. As the phrase indicates, this is a period of time in which positive reinforcers are not available. If the time-out period is made contingent on a particular response, the frequency of that response will decrease.

The most common application of this technique for problem behavior is in controlling tantrums and aggressive behavior. For example, Montrose Wolf, Todd Risley, and Hayden Mees (1964) used a time-out procedure to eliminate tantrums in a 3½-year-old psychotic child named Dicky. Dicky's tantrums included self-destructive behaviors such as head banging and hair pulling.

A comprehensive treatment program to deal with Dicky's other problems required his hospitalization in a children's mental hospital. To deal with the tantrums, the hospital staff was instructed to place Dicky in his room with the door closed contingent upon each tantrum. When the tantrum was over, the door was to be opened. After a period of four months, Dicky's tantrums gradually decreased in severity and finally stopped altogether.

This is a time-out procedure because it deprived Dicky of his usual reinforcers, including social contact and the opportunity to participate in ongoing activities. However, it is clearly more complicated than that. As James Sherman and Donald Baer (1969) have pointed out, this type of time-out procedure may involve four components: (1) As just mentioned, if the environment provides positive reinforcement and time-out deprives the child of this, then the procedure involves response cost. (2) Since time-out is terminated when the child is acting appropriately, the procedure may be reinforcing the more appropriate behavior. (3) Since during the time-out the child is placed in an environment in which people pay no attention to him, and if attention has maintained the child's tantrums, then time-out will provide an opportunity for extinction.

(4) The isolation associated with confinement may be aversive and serve as punishment.

One of the major problems in implementing a time-out procedure is defining the behavior which will result in time-out. When Dicky first started this program, his tantrums included whining, crying, and self-destructive behavior. The criterion for time-out initially was the engaging in any two or more of these behaviors simultaneously. As Dicky improved, the criterion was lowered to include any of these behaviors alone. Not only was the criterion clearly specified, but it was gradually altered so as to require increasingly more appropriate behavior.

Another problem in implementing time-out procedures has to do with social interaction on the way to and from the time-out room. Initially, Dicky's attendants offered elaborate explanations as they escorted him to his room and greeted him with apologies and caresses as he emerged at the end of the time-out period. Perhaps due to this, at the beginning of the third month Dicky began having frequent but short (less than five minutes) tantrums. Two procedural alterations were made to deal with this. First, the attendants' behavior gradually evolved to one of perfunctory escort to Dicky's room. At the end of the time-out period, Dicky's door simply was opened. Second, a minimum time limit of 10 minutes was instituted for the time-out period. After these changes, the short tantrums also dropped out.

It is important to note that there are three aspects of time-out which distinguish it from the common child-rearing practice of "sending a child to his room." First, it is not imposed in anger. Often parents punish their children depending on how they feel at the moment. In contrast, a very specific criterion for time-out was established so that it was contingent on Dicky's behavior and not on the mood of the attendants. Second, time-out is terminated by a change in the child's behavior. Often parents send their child to his or her room for an unspecified period of time and allow the child to rejoin the family unpredictably. The advantages of using termination of time-out to reinforce appropriate behavior are thus lost. Third, once time-out has ended there are no further references to it. The consequence for Dicky's tantrums was time-out; later recriminations have no part in the procedure.

Problems When Using Punishment

Although punishment can be dramatically effective in suppressing behavior, there are a number of difficulties which must be considered. First, the person being punished often tries to escape the contingencies. After all, since punishing stimuli usually are aversive, escaping them is negatively reinforcing. This problem was described in Chapter 2 with regard to a self-control procedure for giving up smoking. The smoker taking a cigarette would receive a shock from an apparatus he was wearing. The problem was that smokers would circumvent the contingencies by not wearing the equipment. Thus, subjects quickly learn to discriminate punishment from nonpunishment and, consequently, suppress the target response only when it is likely that they will be punished.

A second problem with punishment concerns the relationship between the punisher and the person being punished. Through higher-order conditioning the punisher may become associated with the aversiveness of the punishment and also become something to be avoided. In addition, punishment sometimes elicits anger and aggression directed at the person doing the punishing. To avoid these undesirable side effects in a continuing relationship (for example, between parent and child), punishment should be used for the very few problems not easily dealt with by reinforcing incompatible appropriate behaviors.

A third problem is that punishment may result in general response inhibition instead of the selective response suppression desired. To avoid punishment, the subject may stop behaving entirely. For example, criticizing a child who gives a wrong answer because he is not paying attention may not alter the child's attending to the lesson. Instead, the child may become reluctant to answer any questions. This development usually indicates that an alternate response (one that will be reinforced and not punished) has not been specified. The subject knows only what *not* to do and has not learned *what* to do. One of the most important principles in using punishment is to specify an appropriate response which will be reinforced. However, this is not an endorsement of appeasement. For example, if a child is having a tantrum, the parent *should not* promise future rewards (e.g., a special dessert) for good behavior. This reinforces the inappropriate behavior. Instances of inappropriate behavior should be ignored or punished (for tantrums, time out is quite effective). Appropriate behavior should be reinforced when it occurs (verbal approval is usually sufficient).

Aversive Conditioning

In Chapter 4, techniques to reduce anxiety based on classical conditioning were described. This section also deals with classical conditioning; but here, instead of reducing aversion, the techniques are used to create aversion.

A historically important illustration of aversive conditioning was Watson and Rayner's (1920) experiment with Albert (see Chapter 1). In a demonstration of how fears can be conditioned, a classical conditioning procedure was used to change the stimulus value of a rat from desirable to undesirable. Watson and Rayner clearly demonstrated that an aversion to previously desirable stimuli could be created with these techniques.

Alcoholism. This principle was first applied therapeutically with alcoholics in the Soviet Union (Kantorovich, 1930). In the United States, Walter Voegtlin, Frederick Lemere, and their colleagues treated over five thousand alcoholics using aversive conditioning in the late thirties and early forties (e.g., Lemere and Voegtlin, 1950; Voegtlin, Lemere, and Broz, 1940).

The conditioning procedure associated the sight, smell, and taste of alcohol to nausea and vomiting. Conditioning took place in a soundproof room so the patients were not distracted by extraneous stimuli. All that could be heard were the sounds associated with the treatment, such as the liquor being poured and the bottle clinking against the glass.

Vomiting was induced by an injection of emetine in too small a dose to cause vomiting by itself. After the injection, the patient was required to smell, taste, and swallow four ounces of whiskey. This served as a sufficient irritant to the stomach lining, in conjunction with the drug, to induce vomiting. Once vomiting began, the patient drank a glass of near beer containing an emetic to prolong nausea. Each session lasted from 30 minutes to an hour. Patients were typically given four to six sessions over a two-week period.

After the first session, other liquors were introduced for conditioning so that the conditioned response would not be elicited by one particular variety of alcohol alone. At six months and at one year after the initial treatment, patients received one or two booster treatments. In addition, booster treatments were given upon request if a patient felt a desire to resume drinking.

A survey of all patients treated between May, 1935, and October, 1948, found that 44 percent of over four thousand patients had remained totally abstinent after their treatment (Lemere and Voegtlin, 1950). For some of these patients this meant a follow-up period of over 10 years. Of those who relapsed, 878 were treated again, and 39 percent of those remained abstinent. Combining both groups, there was an overall abstinence rate of 51 percent.

Abstinence is a severe criterion for the success of a treatment program. It does not include patients who become moderate or social drinkers and by other standards would be considered successful graduates of the program. Considering the severity of the criterion and the length of the follow-up, the success of this program is quite remarkable. Even so, interest in aversive conditioning waned for about 15 years, and it wasn't until the 1960s that interest again was stimulated. At this time, there were additional reports of the successful use of aversive conditioning for alcoholics (see Rachman and Teasdale, 1969, for a review of these studies).

Sexual deviancy. Besides alcoholism, another major problem area to which aversive conditioning has been applied is sexual deviancy. Although some investigators have used nausea as the UCS, most have considered this impractical. Drug-induced vomiting is very difficult to use. Patients vary in their reaction to the drug, so that it is often difficult to control the important time intervals between CS and UCS. In addition, vomiting limits the number of trials that the patient can be exposed to in any one session. Also, it is a very difficult procedure to use on an outpatient basis, since it requires very close monitoring of the physiological reactions of the patient. Finally, it is messy and unaesthetic! Staff members are reluctant to participate in such a treatment.

Electric shock, an alternative aversive stimulus, has been used successfully and seems to avoid many of the problems of drug-induced vomiting. First, it is possible to quantify and control the intensity and duration of the shock. Second, CS-UCS intervals can be measured precisely. Third, the patient can be given repeated trials during each session. Fourth, it is easily administered on an outpatient basis as it requires fewer personnel; and finally, although painful, it is neat.

One of the most thorough studies using electric shock aversive conditioning was done by Isaac Marks and Michael Gelder (1967) with five male transvestites and fetishists. The particularly noteworthy aspect of this study is that the investigators measured change in the patients during the treatment itself with objective measures. Of these measures, the most important was a piece of equipment constructed to measure penile erection. The equipment consisted of a transducer with a mercury-filled plastic loop which slipped over the shaft of the penis. A 60-unit deflection on the transducer indicated a full erection, while a 10-unit deflection indicated a response that was just barely noticeable to the patient. The equipment was attached by the patient himself and clothes could be worn normally without discomfort. The use of the transducer made it possible to obtain a detailed record of the patient's reactions to a variety of stimuli including photographs, women's clothing, and even their own fantasies.

To illustrate the changes during conditioning, the treatment for one of the patients will be described in detail. He was a 21-year-old, unmarried university student who had been dressing in women's clothing (to achieve sexual excitement) since the age of 13. He had no girlfriends and had never had sexual intercourse.

Before treatment began, in a test situation the patient responded with an erection to seeing and holding women's clothing which he used when he cross-dressed (panties, pyjamas, a skirt, and a slip). He similarly reacted to a photograph of a nude woman which he chose as being particularly sexually stimulating. The first bar graph in Figure 5-4B indicates the amount of erection for each stimulus during this test.

Aversive conditioning sessions were then begun. Shock was applied to either the arm or the leg, and for each session *the patient selected* the shock level so that it was uncomfortable but not severely painful. During each session he was given 20 trials of aversive conditioning with one piece of clothing. On 75 percent of the trials, he received one to three shocks while holding the piece of clothing. Shocks were omitted on the other 25 percent of the trials to increase unpredictability.

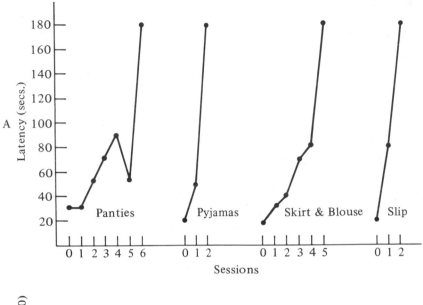

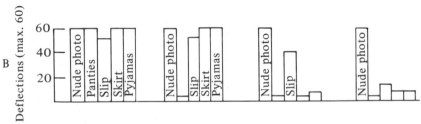

Figure 5-4
Specificity of autonomic changes. (A) Erection latency at end of each
aversion session. (B) Erections after one-minute exposure to stimulus.
(From Marks and Gelder, 1967.)

After six sessions of aversive conditioning to panties, the patient was unable to achieve an erection (see Figure 5-4A). However,
as can be seen in the second bar graph in Figure 5-4B, he was still
being sexually aroused by the other clothing. The results of conditioning were very specific. At each stage of treatment, the patient
would still become sexually aroused by stimuli that had not been
aversively conditioned. In contrast, other patients treated by Marks
and Gelder did show some evidence of generalization. For example,
one of the patients (male, 34, married) had a high-heeled shoe and
boot fetish. Since the age of 12, he masturbated while wearing or

thinking about them. During intercourse with his wife he frequently begged her to kick him. Although treatment was not directed at the patient's masochistic fantasies and desires, they disappeared early in treatment as an aversion was developed to shoes and boots. His wife confirmed the improvement, and also stated that "she enjoyed intercourse more once the patient had ceased asking her to kick him" (p. 721).

Avoidance learning. Although the techniques in this section are negative reinforcement procedures, they are included here for two reasons. First, they were proposed as a refinement of the aversive conditioning procedures just described, and second, their effectiveness may depend more on their classical conditioning elements than the incentive aspects.

In trying to develop an effective conditioning treatment for homosexuality, M. P. Feldman and M. J. MacCulloch (1965) first surveyed the learning literature. They concluded that a potential difficulty with aversive classical conditioning is that the conditioned avoidance might extinguish once the UCS was no longer presented. Since a temporary change in the target behavior is not a desirable outcome, Feldman and MacCulloch sought a procedure likely to result in extreme resistance to extinction. They modeled their techniques after the avoidance learning procedures with dogs described by Richard Solomon and Lyman Wynne (1953).

In Solomon and Wynne's research, a dog was placed in an apparatus that contained compartments separated by a low barrier. Intense electric shock from the floor of the compartment was used as the aversive UCS. The lights of the compartment containing the dog were turned off to serve as the CS for the occurrence of shock. Ten seconds after the lights were turned off the floor was electrified. The dog could escape by jumping over the barrier into the other compartment, and it could avoid the shock altogether if it jumped after the light was turned off and before the 10 seconds had elapsed. If the dog waited until it was shocked before jumping the barrier, this was called an escape trial, and if it jumped within the ten-second interval, this was called an avoidance trial.

Using this procedure, Solomon and Wynne found that dogs quickly learned to jump the barrier to avoid shock. And, particularly important, the jumping response did not extinguish when the shock was disconnected (Solomon, Kamin, and Wynne, 1953). In trial after trial, when the light was turned off, the dog jumped the barrier. The researchers explained the persistence of the response by noting that avoidance learning contained two processes. First, there is a classical conditioning component whereby turning off the light (CS) comes to elicit anxiety (CR) because it has been associated with shock (UCS). Second, there is an instrumental conditioning component in that jumping over the barrier (the avoidance response) is negatively reinforced. During the escape trials, the avoidance response is reinforced because it terminates the shock. Later, during the avoidance and extinction trials, jumping the barrier is still being negatively reinforced, but now because it reduces the anxiety associated with the CS. Because the CS has become aversive, the avoidance response continues to be reinforced.

In Feldman and MacCulloch's procedure, the male homosexual client was told that a picture of an attractive male (previously rated by the client) would be projected on a screen. He was further told that he might receive an electric shock on the leg a few seconds after the picture came on the screen. The client could turn off both the slide and the shock by pressing a switch and, at the same time, saying "No." However, he was instructed to keep the slide on as long as it appeared attractive to him.

In this procedure, then, the picture was the CS and the shock the UCS. The client could avoid the shock by switching the slide off within eight seconds. Pressing the switch while saying "No" was the avoidance response being reinforced. In addition to reinforcing avoidance behavior, Feldman and MacCulloch wanted to reduce the aversiveness of heterosexual stimuli. To do this, they paired a picture of an attractive female (previously rated by the client) with the relief associated with shock offset.

The procedure started with the male slide rated least attractive and the female slide rated most attractive. The first phase continued until the client achieved three successive avoidance trials. Thereafter the same stimuli were reinforced according to a schedule in which one-third of the avoidance responses were ineffective (i.e., the picture stayed on and the client received a shock), one-third of the responses were allowed to succeed (i.e., turn off the slide) immediately, and one-third were allowed to succeed after a delay (but before the entire eight seconds had elapsed). This schedule was followed in order to increase the amount of anxiety associated with male slides. When the client consistently attempted to turn off the slide within two seconds and when he reported indifference or even repulsion, the treatment proceeded to the next stimulus pair. As treatment progressed, increasingly more attractive males and less attractive females were used. Each client received an average of 15 20-minute sessions. In addition, clients received 8 to 10 booster sessions in the year following treatment.

Compared to the aversive conditioning procedures described previously, the problem of generalization in this situation would seem to be overwhelming. First, only pictures of men and women were used as stimuli. For the treatment to be effective, responses learned to the pictures would have to generalize to actual men and women. Second, the avoidance response learned was to press a switch. This response would have to generalize to a wide variety of verbal and motor responses required to avoid homosexual contacts. Third, the *generalized* avoidance response would have to be elicited by the *generalized* conditioned stimuli in situations where the UCS (the shock) had never occurred. This is particularly unlikely given results from avoidance learning experiments conducted with animals (see Herrnstein, 1969). These experiments indicate that the reason the avoidance response in the Solomon and Wynne experiments does not extinguish is that the CS serves as a discriminative cue for the occurrence of the UCS (shock). It is not that the animal is motivated to avoid the CS, but rather that it has not learned that the shock has been turned off. In contrast, the homosexuals do know that they will not be shocked when they are away from the consulting office.

In spite of the theoretical problems, the treatment is effective. Of 43 clients, 25 improved dramatically (with a follow-up period from one to three years), 11 remained unimproved, and 7 failed to complete treatment. Those who improved showed a complete absence of homosexual behavior, had no (or almost no) homosexual fantasies, and either had developed satisfying heterosexual relationships or had active heterosexual fantasies (Feldman and MacCulloch, 1971).

What accounts for this success? It probably is not due to negatively reinforcing the pressing of a switch. The client knows that he is not going to be shocked outside of the treatment room and therefore would have no incentive to engage in avoidance behavior when in the community. In a subsequent comparison of the avoidance and classical conditioning paradigms, Feldman and

MacCulloch (1971) found that the treatments produced equivalent improvement.

It is more likely, then, that the treatment's effectiveness is due to its classical conditioning component. You may recall that the client is told to keep the picture on the screen *as long as it remains attractive*. Thus, not only is the picture associated with pain and anxiety, but so are the client's sexual fantasies about the person pictured. As the sexuality of the pictured males is neutralized, the client is probably less likely to seek out homosexual contacts. In other words, the aversive conditioning only assists the client's commitment to change. If he wished to, he could recondition himself with relatively little effort. All he would need to do is seek out additional homosexual contacts.

The results from aversive conditioning are much more fragile than the popular image, as depicted in novels such as Anthony Burgess's *A Clockwork Orange*. Aversive conditioning can be useful, but only if the client uses the aversion as an aid in changing his behavior. Additionally, most treatments to change sexual orientation do not rely solely on aversive conditioning. Comprehensive programs focus on increasing heterosexual responsiveness in addition to decreasing homosexual arousal. This can be accomplished with a number of procedures described in earlier chapters. For example, if a client were anxious about heterosexual contact, systematic desensitization might be used; if he lacked social skills, behavior rehearsal would be appropriate (see Barlow, 1973, 1974 for a review of additional procedures used in comprehensive treatments for homosexuality).

Treatment of homosexuality also raises ethical issues about the appropriateness of treatment goals. Has the client freely entered treatment, or was he or she coerced into it? Does the very existence of treatments contribute to the continued stigmatization of homosexuals? These and related questions will be discussed in the next chapter.

Smoking. Another illustration of the use of aversive conditioning has been its role in helping people give up smoking. David Schmahl, Edward Lichtenstein, and Darrel Harris (1972) reported good results with a program that required subjects to smoke in unpleasant circumstances. During the treatment sessions, subjects were required to smoke rapidly, inhaling every six seconds. While they did that, additional cigarette smoke and warm air were blown into their faces. They continued rapid smoking under these conditions until they could not stand it any longer. A trial ended when the subject put out his cigarette and said something such as, "I don't want to smoke anymore." The subject endured two or three trials each session, and each trial lasted about three minutes.

Subjects were strongly urged not to smoke between sessions. A subject having an overwhelming desire to have a cigarette was to contact the therapist (at any time of day or night) for an "impromptu" session. Note that the subject's cooperation was required. The aversive conditioning served to assist the subject to maintain the commitment to give up smoking.

Each subject received a total of 14 treatment sessions. At the end of treatment, all subjects were abstinent. This result is not surprising. Almost any treatment decreases the frequency of smoking during the treatment itself—the real test of its effectiveness comes later, during the follow-up period. In this study, 16 of 25 subjects (64 percent) were still abstinent six months later.

Smoking has been one of the most difficult problems to treat. It is not unusual to have success rates as low as 15–20 percent abstinent six months after treatment. Thus, the aversive conditioning was remarkably effective. This high success rate was repeated in a later study (Lichtenstein et al., 1973) in which 18 of 30 subjects (60 percent) were abstinent six months after treatment. These two studies provide convincing evidence that aversive conditioning can be a powerful aid in helping people change their own behavior.

Teaching controlled drinking. An avoidance conditioning paradigm has also been used in a revolutionary program to teach alcoholics to become social drinkers—revolutionary because there is a widely held belief that alcoholics are incapable of social drinking. This belief has been propagated primarily by Alcoholics Anonymous, whose members dedicate themselves to abstinence for fear of losing control of their drinking after even one drink. AA members believe that alcoholism is a disease and that, as a result of it, their bodies have been altered so that they no longer can tolerate alcohol.

The long-term physiological effects of alcohol aside, abstinence may very well be the most efficient treatment goal. It is very difficult to learn to consume anything (for instance, cigarettes, food, or alcohol) in moderation once one is used to consuming it in large quantities. However, there are many benefits to be gained by making social drinking a viable alternative to abstinence. A social drinker would not constantly have to fight yielding to temptation, especially in our society where there are so many inducements to drink. In addition, the social drinker would not have to limit his circle of friends and acquaintances in order to avoid social pressure to have "just one."

Kenneth Mills, Mark Sobell, and Halmuth Schaefer (1971) developed their program using an avoidance conditioning paradigm after determining how alcoholics differ from social drinkers. In a previous study they had found that alcoholics are more likely to prefer straight to mixed drinks, more likely to gulp than sip or nurse their drinks, and that they continue to drink well beyond the point at which a social drinker would stop.

In their avoidance conditioning program, alcoholics were served drinks in a specially constructed bar at Patton State Hospital in California. Gulping, drinking straight drinks, and excessive drinking were punished with electric shock applied to the fingers of the patient's nondominant hand. Sipping, drinking mixed drinks (or beer or wine), and ordering no more than three drinks allowed the patient to avoid shock.

Once the patient had learned to limit his drinking, additional social pressure was put on him to have another drink. The bartender or other people in the bar would say something such as, "Oh, come on, one more won't hurt you." In later sessions, if the patient continued to refuse another drink, a drink would be poured out in front of him and the session would be ended only after the patient left the bar without drinking it.

No attempt was made to program generalization; nevertheless, the setting was quite realistic and the alcohol was real, so some generalization could be expected.

Thirteen alcoholics (average age of 47.5 years, with an average of 6.4 previous hospital admissions for alcoholism) were treated. An additional 13 patients who volunteered for the program but instead received only the usual hospital regimen served as a control group. For 12 months after treatment, both treated and control patients, as well as friends and relatives, were contacted regularly by a social worker who managed to keep track of 10 of the treated patients and 11 of the control patients. One treated patient and 3 control patients were in jail for part of the year and thus not able to drink. Of the rest, Schaefer (1972) reported that 7 of the 9 treated patients were either abstinent or exhibiting controlled drinking while only 2 of the 8 control patients fell into those categories. The others were drinking excessively.

Encouraged by these results, Mark and Linda Sobell (Sobell and Sobell, 1973a) carried out an extensive evaluation of behavioral versus conventional treatment for alcoholics having a treatment goal of either abstinence or social drinking. Seventy male alcoholics hospitalized at Patton State Hospital were treated.

First a decision was made as to the appropriate treatment goal for each alcoholic. Those who requested abstinence as a goal or lacked family support for controlled drinking were assigned to the abstinence condition. Those who requested social drinking, had family support, and/or had practiced social drinking in the past were assigned to the social drinking condition. Then, the men were randomly assigned to either the conventional hospital treatment program or a more comprehensive version of the behavioral program described earlier.

When controlled drinking was the goal, in addition to receiving aversive conditioning, subjects practiced alternative responses to stress and viewed themselves both sober and drunk on video tape. When total abstinence was the goal, the aversive conditioning procedure was modified so that the subject could avoid shock only if he refused the drink entirely. Subjects received continuous shock from the moment they touched the glass until they released it. Abstinence subjects also practiced alternative responses to stress and viewed themselves on video tape.

A very thorough follow-up of graduates of this program was undertaken after they were released from the hospital (Sobell and Sobell, 1973b). Every subject and as many "collateral information sources" as possible were contacted every three to four weeks throughout the follow-up. Collateral sources included friends, relatives, employers, and people at private and public agencies—anyone who might have contact with and knowledge about the subject's drinking. As many as 15 collateral sources were used per subject. From these data, each day of the follow-up was rated as a day on which the subject was (1) abstinent, (2) exhibiting controlled drinking, (3) drunk, or (4) incarcerated.

The results of the study are presented in Figures 5-5 and 5-6.

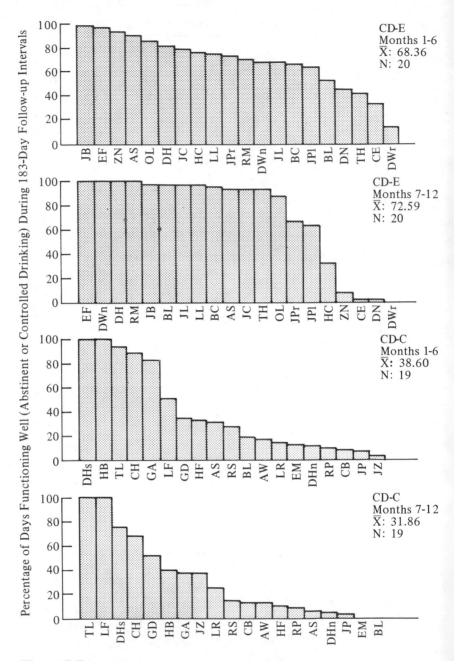

Figure 5-5
Percentage of days spent functioning well (abstinent or controlled drinking) by individual controlled drinker experimental (CD-E) and control (CD-C) subjects during each of two consecutive six-month (183-day) follow-up intervals. (From Sobell and Sobell, 1973b.)

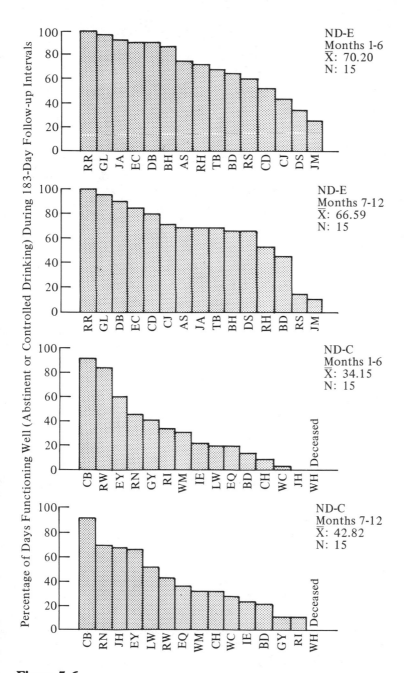

Figure 5-6
Percentage of days spent functioning well (abstinent or controlled drinking) by individual nondrinker experimental (ND-E) and control (ND-C) subjects during each of two consecutive six-month (183-day) follow-up intervals. (From Sobell and Sobell, 1973b.)

As can be seen in Figure 5-5, patients who received the behavior therapy treatment for controlled drinking (CD-E) were functioning well (i.e., were either abstinent or exhibiting controlled drinking) a much higher percentage of the time than patients who also had a controlled drinking goal but received the conventional hospital treatment (CD-C). Similarly, as can be seen in Figure 5-6, patients having a goal of nondrinking who received the behavior therapy treatment (ND-E) functioned well a higher percentage of the time than patients having the same goal but who received the conventional treatment (ND-C).

This study provides rather convincing evidence that it is possible to teach some former alcoholics to be controlled drinkers. The usefulness of this approach will depend, however, on the extent of replication which other investigators in other settings can achieve.

Covert Sensitization

In some of the aversive conditioning studies (e.g., Marks and Gelder, 1967), fantasies and imagined stimuli were used successfully as the CS. An obvious next step would test whether conditioning would take place if an imagined UCS were used. Joseph Cautela (1966, 1967) tried just that when he developed *covert sensitization*, in which the client imagines both the CS and the UCS. For example, if the problem being treated were alcoholism, the patient would imagine tasting and drinking his favorite liquor (the CS) and then imagine becoming nauseated and vomiting (the UCS). The following excerpt is a typical covert sensitization trial:

> You are walking into a bar. You decide to have a glass of beer. You are now walking toward the bar. As you are approaching the bar you have a funny feeling in the pit of your stomach. Your stomach feels all queasy and nauseous. Some liquid comes up your throat and it is very sour. You try to swallow it back down, but as you do this, food particles start coming up your throat to your mouth. You are now reaching the bar and you order a beer. As the bartender is pouring the beer, puke comes up into your mouth. You try to keep your mouth closed and swallow it down. You reach for the glass of beer to wash it down. As soon as your hand touches the glass, you can't hold it down any longer. You have to open your mouth and you puke. It goes all over your hand, all

over the glass and the beer. You can see it floating around in the beer. Snot and mucus come out of your nose. Your shirt and pants are all full of vomit. The bartender has some on his shirt. You notice people looking at you. You get sick again and you vomit some more and more. You turn away from the beer and immediately you start to feel better. As you run out of the barroom, you start to feel better and better. When you get out into clean fresh air you feel wonderful. You go home and clean yourself up (Cautela, 1967, pp. 461–62).[1]

On subsequent trials, other settings and other liquors would be used as the CS. Aversive scenes other than nausea (e.g., seeing a dead body) also could be substituted if imagining nausea was not aversive or if the client began to habituate to its aversiveness.

Using essentially the same procedure, Anant (1967) has reported remarkable results with alcoholics. All 26 of his patients were successfully treated with no relapses (follow-up period from 8 to 15 months). Another study (Ashem and Donner, 1968) found that only 6 of their 15 treated patients (40 percent) were abstinent six months following treatment. However, none of their 8 control patients were abstinent.

Other studies have failed to find dramatic effects for covert sensitization. In one study (Lick and Bootzin, 1971), rather meager results were obtained for the use of covert sensitization as the sole treatment for obesity. Overweight women received four weeks of covert sensitization and returned for a follow-up assessment five weeks later. Over the nine-week period, covert sensitization subjects lost no more weight (an average of only four pounds) than no-treatment control subjects. However, covert sensitization did affect the subjects' ratings of the attractiveness of the target foods. Some subjects, however, continued to eat the target foods even though they rated them as less attractive. Others actually seem to have changed their eating preferences but did not lose weight because they increased their intake of nontarget foods.

[1] When Cautela developed this technique he conceptualized it as a classical conditioning procedure, but later (Cautela, 1969) he stressed the punishment component. Because imagined vomiting is contingent upon imagined behavior it is an imagined punishment procedure. That it is also a punishment procedure does not negate the importance of the classical conditioning component. In covert sensitization, both external stimuli (the bar, sight and smell of liquor) and response-produced stimuli (reaching for, tasting, and swallowing the liquor) are associated with the aversive UCS.

Covert sensitization may not be adequate as the only treatment of overeating, but it can play an important role in a more comprehensive treatment program. For example, Richard Stuart (1967), in his program to help overweight people change their eating habits (see Chapter 2), used covert sensitization selectively for those particular high calorie foods that a client craved and had difficulty giving up. (Also see Mahoney, 1974, for a review of covert sensitization and related techniques.)

Another interesting example of covert sensitization within a larger treatment program has been reported by Gerald Davison (1968). The client was a male, 21-year-old college senior who was concerned about his sadistic sexual fantasies while masturbating. He reported that only sadistic fantasies aroused him. He became quite concerned about this after reading a Freudian account of "sado-masochism," especially since a "poor prognosis" was mentioned. Because he was worried about the content of his fantasies, he avoided dating and felt it impossible to consider marriage. He had not had any homosexual contacts or fantasies.

The treatment had four basic components. First, the client's problem was reinterpreted for him in learning terms. Second, a conditioning program was instituted to increase the capacity of nonsadistic fantasies to result in sexual arousal. Third, covert sensitization was used to decrease the frequency of sadistic fantasies. And fourth, attempts were directed toward increasing his contacts with women.

The first component was introduced because the client was so concerned about the seriousness of his problem. Davison spent most of the first session discussing possible causes of the behavior, stressing the view that deviant behavior follows the same principles as other behavior (and thus can be changed). He cited numerous instances from his own clinical practice of the "liberating effects" observed when people viewed maladaptive behavior as due to "normal" psychological processes instead of "disease" processes.

The second part of the treatment focused on increasing the sexual arousal capacity of nonsadistic fantasies. The client was instructed that, when assured of privacy, he was to obtain an erection by whatever means possible (probably through a sadistic fantasy). Then he was to masturbate while looking at a picture of a nude woman. If he began to lose the erection, he was to use the sadistic fantasy as a way of maintaining it. It was crucial, however, that the client focused on the picture at the moment of climax. As treatment proceeded, the client was instructed to imagine a nude woman while masturbating instead of using the picture.

Although he improved in his ability to reach climax by means of nonsadistic fantasies, he still derived considerable pleasure from sadistic fantasies. Therefore, covert sensitization was used as part three. An aversive image which was particularly effective (as indicated by "grimaces, contortions, and groans") was "a large bowl of 'soup,' composed of steaming urine with reeking fecal boli bobbing around on top" (Davison, 1968, p. 86). First, the client imagined a pretty girl struggling to free herself from stakes in the ground to which she was tied (one of the client's typical fantasies). Then, he imagined drinking the "soup" and becoming nauseated, all the while "peering over the floating debris at the struggling girl." Within two weeks after this session, the client reported that he was unable to obtain an erection to a sadistic fantasy.

The fourth part of the treatment was directed at increasing the client's contacts with women. The client was assigned to ask a woman out on a coffee date and to spend time just looking at women. Following the covert sensitization session, he finally spent time with two women. In fact, he reported an urge to hug one of them (a new experience for him) and began to talk about dating.

One month after therapy terminated, the client reported there had been no recurrence of sadistic fantasies. However, 16 months later, he reported that he purposely began to use sadistic fantasies 6 months after therapy terminated,

. . . resolving to enjoy my fantasies until June 1, and then to reform once more. This I did. On June 1, right on schedule, I bought an issue of *Playboy* and proceeded to give myself the treatment again. Once again, it worked like a charm. In 2 weeks, I was back in my reformed state, where I am now. I have no need for sadistic fantasies. . . . I have also been pursuing a vigorous (well, vigorous for *me*) program of dating. In this way, I have gotten to know a lot of girls of whose existence I was previously only peripherally aware. As you probably know, I was very shy with girls before; well, now I am not one-fifth as shy as I used to be. In fact, by my old standards, I have become a regular rake! [Davison, 1968, p. 89]

Covert sensitization may be an effective alternative to the use of painful aversive stimuli. In addition, it has considerable utility as a self-control procedure. Recently, encouraging results have been reported (Maletzky, 1974) about a method for increasing the effectiveness of covert sensitization.

Assisted covert sensitization. Barry Maletzky calls his procedure "assisted" covert sensitization. While the nausea-inducing scene is being described, an open bottle of valeric acid (a substance which is rather foul-smelling) is placed under the subject's nose.

Maletzky used this procedure in treating 10 exhibitionists. Treatment sessions took place twice a week for about 10 weeks. Toward the end of the treatment, subjects were given a small bottle of valeric acid to take with them and were instructed to sniff it at places which had previously elicited exposing behavior. At 3, 6, and 12 months after treatment, the subjects returned for "booster" sessions.

The results were dramatic. Whereas before treatment, subjects averaged five exhibitionist acts a month, after treatment 9 of 10 subjects did not engage in any acts for the entire 12 months. The tenth subject engaged in only one act. Fantasies about exposure also decreased dramatically.

Assisted covert sensitization appears to have considerable promise, but it too would probably be most effectively applied within more comprehensive treatment programs.

Recommended Readings

Two excellent sources which cover material related to that discussed in this chapter are:

BUCHER, B., & LOVAAS, O. I. Use of aversive stimulation in behavior modification. In M. R. Jones (Ed.), *Miami symposium on the prediction of behavior, 1967: Aversive stimulation.* Coral Gables: University of Miami Press, 1968.

RACHMAN, S., & TEASDALE, J. *Aversion therapy and behaviour disorders: An analysis.* Coral Gables: University of Miami Press, 1969.

6

Philosophical and Ethical Issues

The preceding chapters document the explosion of interest and activity that has taken place in behavior therapy in the past 15 years. A bewildering array of techniques has been applied to an ever-increasing range of problems. The process of evaluation and refinement is by no means over. The data relating to many techniques only hint at their promise—more rigorous evaluations will be required.

Along with its increasing popularity, behavior therapy has become increasingly controversial. As mentioned in Chapter 1, much of the controversy is due to a misunderstanding of what is and what is not behavior modification. Over and over again techniques such as psychosurgery, drug treatments, and electroconvulsive shock treatment (ECT) are mistakenly included under the term *behavior modification*, whereas other procedures which purport to change behavior—such as psychotherapy, education, religion, and love—are not.

The popular and negative image of the product of a behavior modification treatment seems to be something similar to a mindless automaton who responds only to the commands of its masters. It is hoped that the previous chapters provide sufficient refutation of this notion. Indeed, behavior therapy could be more accurately described as directed toward self-control. Even aversive conditioning techniques are only a means of assisting people in changing their own behavior. Far from being automatic, the results of aversive conditioning are often fragile and can be undermined rather easily.

THE ROLE OF THOUGHTS AND FEELINGS

Some of the uneasiness about behavior modification results from the emphasis upon changing behavior by altering external consequences. Critics have argued that people are not passive responders to external events; rather, they have feelings and ideas and can choose among alternative courses of action. To these critics, behavior modification implies a "mechanistic" model of humanity in which people are little more than robots (albeit very complicated ones).

Central to this objection is the role of internal events (such as thoughts and feelings). The issue with regard to thoughts and feelings is not whether they exist, but whether they play an important causal role in the occurrence of behavior. No behavior modifier denies the existence of internal events. However, some feel that internal events play, at best, a minor role in determining subsequent behavior.

Perhaps the strongest position has been taken by B. F. Skinner (1971), who states that internal events can be ignored in an analysis of behavior because they are byproducts of external, observable events. Notice that Skinner does not deny their existence—but rather their importance. An illustration of this point is the typical answer to the question, "Why are you going to the theater?" Usually the theater-goer says that he "feels" like going. For Skinner, this "feeling" to go to the theater is a byproduct of previous reinforcement. Thus, it would be more to the point to ask what happened the last time the person went to the theater. Since it is possible to predict the person's behavior from previous reinforcing events, it is Skinner's position that internal events can be safely ignored.

Although operant procedures that focus only on observable behavior have been very successful (see Chapter 3), most behavior modifiers have not followed Skinner's suggestion to ignore internal events. Instead, many acknowledge that cognitive or symbolic activities can affect overt behavior. Procedures such as systematic desensitization, implosive therapy, and covert sensitization all use internal events (e.g., imagining a feared object) to alter subsequent behavior.

However, thinking and other internal processes are not viewed as "autonomous" by behavior therapists, but rather as covert responses which can be affected by the application of learning principles just as external or overt responses can. For example, it is possible to develop treatments for increasing or decreasing the frequency of particular thoughts just as it is possible to increase or decrease overt behavior. Meichenbaum's work in teaching new self-statements to clients (see Chapter 4) is a superb example of this process. There is a sizeable body of behavior modification research and practice which, similar to Meichenbaum's research, is focused on helping clients develop new cognitive strategies for dealing with their environment (e.g., see Mahoney's *Cognition and Behavior Modification,* 1974). Far from denying the existence of internal events or even ignoring them, behavior therapists have developed demonstrably effective treatments using symbolic control.

Control Is Not Coercion

The fear that behavior is being controlled is frequently connected to behavior modification. In the usual sense of the word *control,* this is not true. No one is coerced or forced to behave in a particular way. Instead, control is used by behavior modifiers to mean predictability or lawfulness. A little girl learning to ride a bicycle is exhibiting lawful behavior. She will gradually eliminate those responses that lead to falling down and will increase the frequency of responses that keep her balanced. Her behavior is being "controlled" by its consequences, but she is not coerced into behaving that way.

Unethical programs. Although there is nothing intrinsically coercive about behavior modification, some coercive programs have been implemented that call themselves "behavior modification" programs. Coercive programs are a particular danger within total institutions such as prisons and mental hospitals where administrators have considerable power over the quality of residents' lives. Punitive and severe deprivations could be instituted and "justified" by applying behavior modification jargon.

Two such programs which have received considerable noto-
riety are worth describing in detail. The first involved an American
psychiatrist who, while on a two-month tour of duty in South Viet-
nam, helped set up a program to get hospitalized mental patients
working and, eventually, out of the hospital (Cotter, 1967). To
do this, he gave electroconvulsive shock treatments (ECT) to all
patients (irrespective of diagnosis) who refused to work. Cotter,
with the help of two Vietnamese psychiatrists, administered several
thousand electroconvulsive shock treatments. On wards in which
ECT was not effective, patients were told that they could not eat
unless they worked. Most underwent only mild deprivation, but
some patients went three days without food before they "volunteered" to work.

As patients became ready for discharge, Cotter faced the additional problem of what to do with those who did not have relatives
to whom they could be discharged. This problem was solved by
volunteering their services to Special Forces as agriculture teams.
These 10-man teams were shipped into Viet Cong territory where
they tended crops in enclaves controlled by American troops.
Growing crops at these enclaves cut the cost of having to ship
food to the enclaves.

Cotter completely ignored the political context in which his
program operated and justified his treatment program on the
grounds that it was effective. Effectiveness is not a sufficient ethical
standard. As David Begelman (1975) has pointed out,

> the ethical propriety of Cotter's program is no more guaranteed
> to spring from his professed allegiance to results and operant
> theory than is the whipping of black slaves by plantation-owners
> justified by empirical evidence that such methods are in demon-
> strable service of increasing work productivity.

The second program was conducted with mentally ill prisoners
at the Iowa Security Medical Facility. Inmates with "behavior
problems" received injections of apomorphine (a drug which in-
duces vomiting lasting about 15 minutes) for rule violations. The
drug could be injected for violations such as "not getting up, for
giving cigarettes against orders, for talking, for swearing, or for
lying" (*Knecht v. Gillman*, 1973). Violations were reported by
other inmates and members of the staff.

This program was "justified" by its administrators as an application of aversive conditioning. Presumably, an aversion to being uncooperative was being conditioned. That seems rather unlikely, given the arbitrariness of what was labeled as "uncooperative" and the wide fluctuations in the interval between actual violation and nausea. The program might have been effective in reducing violations within the institution, but not because a conditioned aversion was produced—rather, because the inmates were rather severely punished for violations. And as one expert witness testified, the use of apomorphine for rule violations was punishment that was worse than a controlled beating since the drug could not be controlled once it was administered.

In *Knecht v. Gillman,* the United States Court of Appeals for the Eighth Circuit ruled that this treatment constituted "cruel and unusual punishment" unless the treatment was administered to an inmate who "knowingly and intelligently" consented to it. The court stated certain conditions to ensure that informed consent would be obtained before inmates participated in the program and that they would be able to withdraw consent at any time. The court did not rule on whether this was an appropriate program for those who consented to it.

These two programs horrify behavior therapists just as they do the general public. They do not represent the way in which behavior modification is typically employed. Abusive, coercive programs occasionally occur, and patients and inmates have the right to be protected from them. This would be the case no matter how the program was justified—whether in behavior modification language or in language based on some other conceptual framework.

Informed consent in prisons. As pointed out in Chapter 3, the safeguard of informed consent within prisons may not be sufficient. Prisoners may consent to participate in prison-sponsored programs on the expectation of special privileges or out of fear of reprisals. Because of this concern, some have objected to and would prohibit any behavior modification programs within the prisons that use aversive stimulation whether or not consent of those participating is obtained.

Such a prohibition might deprive some prisoners of programs that would have aided their adjustment when returned to the community. For example, an aversive conditioning program at Somers

State Prison, Connecticut, was developed for inmates convicted for molesting children. Child molesters are despised by the rest of the prison population, so life within the prison is somewhat harsher for them than it is for other prisoners.

Aversive conditioning treatment was offered to 45 eligible inmates, of whom 12 volunteered. The treatment was modeled after the Feldman and MacCulloch procedure (see Chapter 5). Painful electric shocks delivered to the upper thigh were associated with presentations of slides of children, and slides of adults signaled no shock. Inmates in the program have been enthusiastic about the results. Although 7 of the 12 have been returned to their communities, follow-up data are not yet available.

Nevertheless, the Connecticut Civil Liberties Union objected to this program and any other behavior modification programs which "are intended to alter personal values or personalities of inmates through the means of chemotherapy, surgery, electroshock and the like." [1] The error in the definition of behavior modification aside, the Civil Liberties Union is willing to sacrifice potentially good programs in order to ensure that inmates are protected from programs similar to the Iowa one.

An alternative to a blanket prohibition is to provide mechanisms so that institutional programs can be evaluated and abuses eliminated. Kassirer (1974) suggested that programs for large institutional populations might be reviewed by a committee composed of both those with scientific and medical competence and those competent to judge ethical, moral, and legal implications. Additionally, an ombudsman system, independent of the administrative chain of command, could be instituted to ensure that inmates' complaints were receiving due consideration. Some set of guidelines and system for evaluation and review is necessary. But it is also important to allow for the development of programs from which inmates would benefit and which they would voluntarily seek out.

THE USE OF AVERSIVE STIMULI

The use of aversive stimuli even when seemingly appropriate has been the basis for another indictment of all behavior modification. Implicit in this criticism is that behavior therapists are sadistic

[1] The Brief, Nov. 1974, p. 6. Published by the Illinois Division of the American Civil Liberties Union.

and power hungry. It is unlikely that behavior therapists are any less dedicated and humane than any other group of therapists. In fact, aversive methods compose only a very small proportion of the techniques available to and in use by behavior therapists. New techniques such as covert sensitization, assisted covert sensitization, and the use of lemon juice as an aversive stimulus are constantly being explored as alternatives to those instances in which more painful stimulation has been required.

No one is more aware of the disadvantages of aversive stimulation than are behavior therapists. In Chapter 5, many of the disadvantages were enumerated. Usually, alternative techniques had been tried without effect before aversive stimulation was used; but even so, the disadvantages were carefully weighed against the advantages in each instance before proceeding. Although there are problems and disadvantages in using aversive stimulation, it is sometimes the only effective procedure.

An excellent illustration of its effectiveness was Lovaas's use of electric shock to suppress self-destructive behavior in psychotic children. The ethical question, given an effective but painful treatment, is whether it is more humane to leave a child in restraints for months and maybe years than to administer a few painful shocks. To extend the argument even further, a prohibition against effective but painful treatments would mean doing without inoculations, surgery, dentistry, and so forth.

The above arguments should not be interpreted to mean that there are no ethical dilemmas if one has effective treatments. As mentioned earlier, there are some ethical considerations that are independent of effectiveness. For example, forcing a claustrophobic to remain in a small room may eventually extinguish his anxiety. If the patient had not consented to the treatment, whether or not it was effective, most of us would view that procedure as unethical. If, however, the patient had consented, most of us would view it as ethical even if the patient experienced discomfort initially. The issue is not the aversiveness of the procedure, but rather whether the treatment was applied within a framework of informed consent.

Issues Related to Consent

An important component of the preceding discussion is the implication that the client has sought out and consents to treatment. What about those instances in which the client does not consent to treatment? Basically, this is an issue of whether the therapist is acting for the client or for society. In the vast majority of cases, the interests of both coincide so there is no conflict. Even in most of the cases in which the client's consent is not sought (e.g., teaching autistic children to talk, suppressing an infant's vomiting), there is little conflict. In these particular instances, the client is not able to consent meaningfully and someone (e.g., a parent or guardian) with the legal and moral responsibility seeks out and consents to treatment.

A more troublesome problem arises in connection with people who become the responsibility of the State by being imprisoned or committed to a mental hospital. Here it is most likely that therapists employed by an institution will see themselves primarily as agents of society since their activities are affected by institutional policy. Because of this, some (e.g., Thomas Szasz, 1963) argue that therapists have no business working for the State. It is their view that it is not possible to balance the interests of the client and those of the State, and therefore therapists should work only with those who freely have sought their help. Many behavior therapists advocate this position as well.

Clearly this is not the position taken by those who actually work within institutions. They are more likely to see themselves as acting in the interests of both the individual and society. Even inside an institution, it is possible to maximize voluntary consent and participation in treatment. Significant movement in the direction of client participation in both the setting of goals and the day-to-day administration of programs has already occurred. Examples of this include client-administered token economies and Fairweather's group program which placed considerable responsibility for decision making on the patients themselves.

VALUE ISSUES

Pointing to ways of maximizing consent within institutions only sidesteps the issue raised by Szasz. As mentioned above, the issue ultimately becomes whether the therapist is acting in the interests of the client or in the interests of society. Szasz stresses that a therapist's only allegiance is to the client. In an excellent discussion of this issue, Leonard Krasner (1969) points out that all therapists act according to their own values, which are themselves determined by the society of which they are a part. Take the example of a therapist who insists that his own values play no role because he has helped a client reduce anxiety associated with an extramarital affair even though the therapist values marital fidelity. What the therapist does not recognize is that he still is acting according to an important societal value: to allow others to act as they wish within certain bounds. To push the therapist to the ethical dilemma, we would have to ask how he would deal with someone who wished to act outside the boundaries set by society. For example, how would the therapist deal with a professional murderer who seeks help to reduce the anxiety associated with killing someone? Although it is possible to devise a treatment plan for such a problem, it is inconceivable that a therapist holding the values of the larger society would carry out the treatment. That is not to say that a willing therapist could not be found, but it would require someone with values different from those of most of us.

Although behavior modifiers act according to the values of society, that does not mean that they must be "tools of the establishment" or defenders of the status quo. First, the therapist, like anyone else, plays a role in changing the values of society. In addition, when there is conflict within the society over a particular issue, there will be therapists on both sides. The techniques available to the behavior modifier can be applied in the service of widely different values. No set of values concerning the appropriateness of particular goals is part and parcel of the techniques.

Homosexuality. An examination of the issues involved in the treatment of homosexuality may further illustrate this. In December, 1973, the board of trustees of the American Psychiatric Association voted to remove homosexuality from the list of "mental disorders" contained in its *Diagnostic and Statistical Manual of Mental Disorders*. Behavior therapists, for the most part, applauded the decision. In fact, in 1974 the Association for the Advancement of Behavior Therapy released its own statement affirming that homosexuality, as one of the many expressions of human sexuality, was not in itself a sign of behavior pathology.

Behavior therapists have prided themselves on the fact that the client determines the goals for treatment. For example, a homosexual who comes to a behavior therapist for help in becoming heterosexual could receive such help. At the same time, a homosexual who would like to reduce the anxiety and guilt associated with being homosexual but does not want to change his sexual preference could also receive treatment. As pointed out earlier, no set of values concerning the appropriateness of particular goals is a fundamental part of behavioral techniques.

Gay Liberation spokesmen, however, object to the very existence of treatments for homosexuality on the grounds that they legitimize society's continued stigmatization of homosexuals. And if homosexuals were not stigmatized, they state, it would be unlikely that a homosexual would desire treatment to change his or her sexual orientation. Homosexuals would still have a number of problems and stresses associated with daily living, just as heterosexuals do, but those could be dealt with independently of the client's sexual orientation.

This position has won advocates among some behavior therapists. For example, Gerald Davison in his Presidential Address at the annual convention of the Association for the Advancement of Behavior Therapy (1974) called upon behavior therapists to "stop engaging in voluntary therapy programs aimed at altering the choice of adult partners to whom . . . clients are attracted." He pointed out that when homosexuals seek out help to change sexual orientation it is to escape the abuse heaped upon them by society. Providing treatments legitimizes the stigma. Further, Begelman (1975) has suggested that instead of treating homosexuality, behavior therapists should "make strides in the resolution of the real 'problem': the public derogation of diverse life styles."

On issues requiring value decisions, there is not going to be unanimity among behavior therapists. Some will continue to offer homosexuals treatment to change their sexual orientation. To them, the link between the availability of treatment and society's continued stigmatization may appear rather remote. And they are likely to decide that the immediate needs of the client, whose desire to change may be quite sincere, take precedence over long-term social goals.

There is nothing in a behavior therapy technology which suggests how such value decisions should be resolved. However, behavior therapists, as members of the community at large, will participate in the evolution of society's values. As society's values change, so will the desirability of some treatment goals.

Recommended Reading

BEGELMAN, D. A. Ethical and legal issues of behavior modification. In M. Hersen, R. Eisler, and P. Miller (Eds.), *Progress in behavior modification.* Vol. 1. New York: Academic Press, 1975.

Glossary

ABA design Experimental design in which treatment is alternately presented (the A periods) and withdrawn or reversed (the B periods). If the subject improves every time a treatment begins, and relapses every time treatment is withdrawn, a functional relationship has been demonstrated between treatment and improvement.

Anxiety hierarchy A series of anxiety-producing situations arranged from least to most anxiety arousing

Aversive conditioning A classical conditioning procedure to reduce the desirability of stimuli by repeatedly pairing them with an aversive unconditioned stimulus

Avoidance learning A procedure in which responses that avoid or escape an aversive stimulus are negatively reinforced

Baseline Pretreatment period during which the frequency of the target response is recorded

Behavior modification The attempt to apply learning and other experimentally derived psychological principles to problem behavior

Behavior rehearsal Technique in which the desired behavior (e.g., assertive behavior) is practiced until it can be performed easily and comfortably. It usually involves a combination of modeling, instruction, and practice.

Behavior therapy *See* Behavior modification

Behavioral contract A negotiated agreement which specifies the consequences which will follow the performance of particular behaviors

Case study The description of techniques as applied to one subject. Evidence of the effectiveness of the techniques cannot be considered conclusive, since alternative explanations cannot be ruled out.

159

Classical conditioning The paired presentation of a neutral stimulus (the conditioned stimulus) with a stimulus that reflexively elicits a response (the unconditioned stimulus). By repeated pairing, the neutral stimulus becomes conditioned to elicit a response (the conditioned response) similar to the one elicited by the unconditioned stimulus.

Conditioned reinforcer Stimuli which have been associated with and signal the future delivery of other reinforcers

Conditioned response (CR) *See* Classical conditioning

Conditioned stimulus (CS) *See* Classical conditioning

Contact desensitization *In vivo* treatment for anxiety reduction in which the therapist models the appropriate behavior and then guides the subject through each step of the anxiety hierarchy

Contingency contracting *See* Behavioral contract

Contingency management Changing a response or behavior by controlling its consequences

Contingent reinforcement Reinforcement delivered contingent upon the performance of a specific response

Covert sensitization Aversive conditioning procedure in which the subject imagines both the conditioned and unconditioned stimuli

Discriminative stimuli Cues which signal that reinforcement will be delivered if a particular response is emitted

Echolalia Inappropriate use of language. The person will imitate sentences heard but not use speech to communicate.

Electroconvulsive shock treatment Use of electricity to produce convulsions and unconsciousness. Sometimes used as a treatment for psychotic depression. It is not the same as painful electric shock applied to the extremities; nor is it a behavior modification procedure.

Extinction A process in which a conditioned response is reduced to its preconditioned level. In classical conditioning, the conditioned stimulus is no longer followed by the unconditioned stimulus. In instrumental or operant conditioning, previously reinforced responses are no longer reinforced.

Flooding Rapid *in vivo* exposure to anxiety-eliciting stimuli. Repeated exposure should lead to fear extinction.

Functional analysis Thorough analysis of the frequency of particular behaviors, the situations in which they occur, and their consequences. It is an attempt to discover causal relationships between environmental events and the response of interest.

Generalization *See* Response generalization *and* Stimulus generalization

Habituation Repeated elicitation which leads to a weakening of the response

Implosive therapy A procedure in which the subject's anxiety is maximized and prolonged as a means of extinguishing the anxiety conditioned to images and thoughts of feared events

Instrumental conditioning A type of learning in which response patterns are altered depending upon their consequences

Intermittent reinforcement Any schedule of reinforcement in which the response is not reinforced each time it is performed

Negative reinforcement The process in which the omission or termination of a stimulus increases the frequency of the preceding response

Noncontingent reinforcement Reinforcement which is delivered irrespective of the response performed

Operant conditioning A type of learning in which response patterns are altered depending upon their consequences

Positive reinforcement Presentation of a stimulus which increases the frequency of the response it follows

Premack Principle Any high-probability behavior can be used to reinforce a low-probability behavior

Punishment Presentation of a stimulus which decreases the frequency of the response it follows. *See also* Response cost.

Reinforcement *See* Negative reinforcement *and* Positive reinforcement

Response cost A punishment procedure in which the omission or termination of a stimulus decreases the frequency of the preceding response

Response generalization The spread of effects to responses that were not themselves directly reinforced

Self-monitoring Assessing or recording one's own behavior. Often, this procedure alone causes changes in the target behavior.

Shaping Developing a complex response by reinforcing successive approximations of the final response

Stimulus control Process by which discriminative stimuli for the delivery of reinforcement become highly valid predictors of whether the response will occur

Stimulus generalization A transfer of treatment effects to other stimulus conditions or situations

Stimulus satiation Concept based on the fact that a stimulus is less reinforcing if it is continually available

Successive approximations Responses which increasingly resemble the complex response being shaped. *See also* Shaping.

Time-out from reinforcement A punishment procedure in which the opportunity to receive positive reinforcement is removed

Token A tangible conditioned reinforcer

Token economy An entire environment (e.g., a ward or classroom)

engineered so that appropriate behavior is reinforced with tokens and inappropriate behavior extinguished

Unconditioned response (UCR) A reflexive response elicited by an unconditioned stimulus. *See also* Classical conditioning.

Unconditioned stimulus (UCS) A stimulus which elicits a reflexive response. *See also* Classical conditioning.

Vicarious extinction Process in which emotional responses are extinguished by repeatedly observing that feared performance does not lead to unfavorable consequences

Vicarious reinforcement The reinforcing effects on an observer who witnesses another person being reinforced

References

ANANT, S. S. A note on the treatment of alcoholics by the verbal aversion technique. *Canadian Psychologist,* 1967, *8a,* 19–22.

ASHEM, B., & DONNER, L. Covert sensitization with alcoholics: A controlled replication. *Behaviour Research and Therapy,* 1968, *6,* 7–12.

ATTHOWE, J. M., JR., & KRASNER, L. A preliminary report on the application of contingent reinforcement procedures (token economy) on a "chronic" psychiatric ward. *Journal of Abnormal Psychology,* 1968, *73,* 37–43.

AYLLON, T. Intensive treatment of psychotic behavior by stimulus satiation and food reinforcement. *Behaviour Research and Therapy,* 1963, *1,* 53–61.

AYLLON, T., & AZRIN, N. H. The measurement and reinforcement of behavior of psychotics. *Journal of the Experimental Analysis of Behavior,* 1965, *8,* 357–383.

AYLLON, T., & AZRIN, N. H. *The token economy: A motivational system for therapy and rehabilitation.* New York: Appleton-Century-Crofts, 1968.

AZRIN, N. H., & HOLZ, W. C. Punishment. In W. K. Honig (Ed.), *Operant behavior: Areas of research and application.* New York: Appleton-Century-Crofts, 1966.

BAER, D. M. Laboratory control of thumbsucking by withdrawal and representation of reinforcement. *Journal of the Experimental Analysis of Behavior,* 1962, *5,* 525–528.

BANDURA, A. *Principles of behavior modification.* New York: Holt, Rinehart and Winston, 1969.

BANDURA, A. Psychotherapy based upon modeling principles. In A.

Bergin and S. Garfield (Eds.), *Handbook of psychotherapy and behavior change.* New York: Wiley, 1971.

BANDURA, A., & BARAB, P. Processes governing disinhibitory effects through symbolic modeling. *Journal of Abnormal Psychology,* 1973, *82,* 1–10.

BANDURA, A., BLANCHARD, E. B., & RITTER, B. The relative efficacy of desensitization and modeling approaches for inducing behavioral, affective, and attitudinal changes. *Journal of Personality and Social Psychology,* 1969, *13,* 173–199.

BANDURA, A., GRUSEC, J. E., & MENLOVE, F. L. Vicarious extinction of avoidance behavior. *Journal of Personality and Social Psychology,* 1967, *5,* 16–23.

BARLOW, D. Increasing heterosexual responsiveness in the treatment of sexual deviation: A review of the clinical and experimental evidence. *Behavior Therapy,* 1973, *4,* 655–672.

BARLOW, D. H. The treatment of sexual deviation: Towards a comprehensive behavioral approach. In K. Calhoun, H. Adams, and K. Mitchell (Eds.), *Innovative treatment methods in psychopathology.* New York: Wiley, 1974.

BARRETT, C. L. Systematic desensitization versus implosive therapy. *Journal of Abnormal Psychology,* 1969, *74,* 587–593.

BECKER, W. C., MADSEN, C. H., ARNOLD, C., & THOMAS, D. R. The contingent use of teacher attention and praise in reducing classroom behavior problems. *Journal of Special Education,* 1967, *1,* 287–307.

BEGELMAN, D. A. The ethics of behavioral control and a new mythology. *Psychotherapy: Theory, Research and Practice,* 1971, *8,* 165–169.

BEGELMAN, D. A. Ethical and legal issues of behavior modification. In M. Hersen, R. Eisler, and P. Miller (Eds.), *Progress in behavior modification.* Vol. 1. New York: Academic Press, 1975.

BING, E. *Six practical lessons to an easy childbirth.* New York: Grosset & Dunlap, 1967.

BLANCHARD, E.. B., & YOUNG, L. D. Clinical applications of biofeedback training. *Archives of General Psychiatry,* 1974, *30,* 573–589.

BOOTZIN, R. R. Vomiting as an anxiety response treated by systematic desensitization. Unpublished paper, Northwestern University, 1968.

BOOTZIN, R. A stimulus control treatment for insomnia. *Proceedings of the American Psychological Association,* 1972, *1,* 395–396.

BOOTZIN, R. A stimulus control treatment of insomnia. In P. Hauri (Chairman), *The treatment of sleep disorders.* Symposium presented at the Annual Meeting of the American Psychological Association, Montreal, 1973.

BOOTZIN, R., & KAZDIN, A. A comparison of systematic desensitization with systematic habituation for fear of heights. Paper presented at the Annual Meeting of the Midwestern Psychological Association, Cleveland, 1972.

BUCHER, B., & LOVAAS, O. I. Use of aversive stimulation in behavior modification. In M. R. Jones (Ed.), *Miami Symposium on the Prediction of Behavior, 1967: Aversive Stimulation*. Coral Gables: University of Miami Press, 1968.

BUDZYNSKI, T., STOYVA, J., ADLER, C., & MULLANEY, D. EMG biofeedback and tension headache: A controlled outcome study. *Psychosomatic Medicine*, 1973, *35*, 484–496.

CAUTELA, J. R. Treatment of compulsive behavior by covert sensitization. *Psychological Record*, 1966, *16*, 33–41.

CAUTELA, J. R. Covert sensitization. *Psychological Record*, 1967, *20*, 459–468.

CAUTELA, J. R. Behavior therapy and self-control: Techniques and implications. In C. M. Franks (Ed.), *Behavior therapy: Appraisal and status*. New York: McGraw-Hill, 1969. Pp. 323–340.

COTTER, L. H. Operant conditioning in a Vietnamese mental hospital. *American Journal of Psychiatry*, 1967, *124*, 23–28.

DAVISON, G. C. Elimination of a sadistic fantasy by a client-controlled counterconditioning technique: A case study. *Journal of Abnormal and Social Psychology*, 1968, *73*, 84–90.

DAVISON, G. C. Homosexuality: The ethical challenge. Presidential Address, Annual Convention of the Association for the Advancement of Behavior Therapy, Chicago, 1974.

DAVISON, G. C., & STUART, R. B. Behavior modification and civil liberties. Paper presented at Biennial Conference of the American Civil Liberties Union, Milwaukee, 1974.

D'ZURILLA, T., WILSON, G., & NELSON, R. A preliminary study of the effectiveness of graduated prolonged exposure in the treatment of irrational fear. *Behavior Therapy*, 1973, *4*, 672–685.

ELLIOTT, R., & TIGHE, T. J. Breaking the cigarette habit: A technique involving threatened loss of money. *Psychological Record*, 1968, *18*, 503–513.

FAIRWEATHER, G. W., SANDERS, D. H., MAYNARD, H., & CRESSLER, D. L. *Community life for the mentally ill: An alternative to institutional care*. Chicago: Aldine, 1969.

FELDMAN, M. P. Aversion therapy for sexual deviations: A critical review. *Psychological Bulletin*, 1966, *65*, 65–79.

FELDMAN, M. P., & MACCULLOCH, M. J. The application of anticipatory avoidance learning to the treatment of homosexuality: I. Theory, technique and preliminary results. *Behaviour Research and Therapy,* 1965, *2,* 165–183.

FELDMAN, P., & MacCULLOCH, M. J. *Homosexual behavior: Therapy and Assessment.* New York: Pergamon, 1971.

FERSTER, C. B., NURNBERGER, J. I., & LEVITT, E. B. The control of eating. *Journal of Mathetics,* 1962, *1,* 87–109.

FOXX, R. M., & AZRIN, N. H. Restitution: A method of eliminating aggressive-disruptive behavior of retarded and brain damaged patients. *Behaviour Research and Therapy,* 1972, *10,* 15–29.

FOXX, R. M., & AZRIN, N. H. Dry pants: A rapid method for toilet training children. *Behaviour Research and Therapy,* 1973, *11,* 435–442.

GEER, J. H. Phobia treated by reciprocal inhibition. *Journal of Abnormal and Social Psychology,* 1964, *69,* 642–645.

GOLDIAMOND, I. Self-control procedures in personal behavior problems. *Psychological Reports,* 1965, *17,* 851–868.

GOLDIAMOND, I. Toward a constructional approach to social problems: Ethical and constitutional issues raised by applied behavior analysis. *Behaviorism: A Forum for Critical Discussion,* 1974, *2,* 1–84.

GRAUBARD, P., & ROSENBERG, H. *Classrooms that work.* New York: Dutton, 1974.

HERRNSTEIN, R. J. Method and theory in the study of avoidance. *Psychological Review,* 1969, *76,* 49–69.

HERSEN, M., EISLER, R., & MILLER, P. An experimental analysis of generalization in assertive training. *Behaviour Research and Therapy,* 1974, *12,* 295–310.

HERSEN, M., EISLER, R., MILLER, P., JOHNSON, M., & PINKSTON, S. Effect of practice, instructions, and modeling on components of assertive behavior. *Behaviour Research and Therapy,* 1973, *11,* 443–451.

HODGSON, R., RACHMAN, S., & MARKS, I. The treatment of chronic obsessive-compulsive neurosis: Follow-up and further findings. *Behaviour Research and Therapy,* 1972, *10,* 181–189.

HOGAN, R. A. The implosive technique. *Behaviour Research and Therapy,* 1968, *6,* 423–431.

HOMME, L. *How to use contingency contracting in the classroom.* Champaign, Ill.: Research Press, 1969.

ISAACS, W., THOMAS, J., & GOLDIAMOND, I. Application of operant conditioning to reinstate verbal behavior in psychotics. *Journal of Speech and Hearing Disorders,* 1960, *25,* 8–12.

JACOBSON, E. *Progressive relaxation.* Chicago: University of Chicago Press, 1938.

JACOBSON, E. *Anxiety and tension control.* Philadelphia: Lippincott, 1964.

JONES, M. C. The elimination of children's fears. *Journal of Experimental Psychology,* 1924, *7,* 382–390.

KAHN, M., BAKER, B., & WEISS, J. Treatment of insomnia by relaxation. *Journal of Abnormal Psychology,* 1968, *73,* 556–558.

KANFER, F., & PHILLIPS, J. S. *Learning foundations of behavior therapy.* New York: Wiley, 1970.

KANTOROVICH, N. An attempt at associative-reflex therapy in alcoholism. *Psychological Abstracts,* 1930, *4,* 493.

KASSIRER, L. B. Behavior modification for patients and prisoners: Constitutional ramifications of enforced therapy. *Journal of Psychiatry and Law,* 1974, 245–302.

KAZDIN, A. E. The effect of response cost in suppressing behavior in a pre-psychotic retardate. *Journal of Behavior Therapy and Experimental Psychiatry,* 1971, *2,* 137–141.

KAZDIN, A. E. Self-monitoring and behavior change. In M. J. Mahoney and C. E. Thoresen (Eds.), *Self-control: Power to the person.* Monterey, Calif.: Brooks/Cole, 1974.

KAZDIN, A. E., & BOOTZIN, R. R. The token economy: An evaluative review. *Journal of Applied Behavior Analysis,* 1972, *5,* 343–372.

KELLER, F. S. "Good-bye, teacher . . ." *Journal of Applied Behavior Analysis,* 1968, *1,* 79–89.

KEUTZER, C. S. Behavior modification of smoking: The experimental investigation of diverse techniques. *Behaviour Research and Therapy,* 1968, *6,* 137–157.

Knecht v. Gillman. 488 F.2d 1136, 1139 (8th Cir. 1973).

KRASNER, L. Behavior modification—values and training: The perspective of a psychologist. In C. M. Franks (Ed.), *Behavior therapy: Appraisal and status.* New York: McGraw-Hill, 1969. Pp. 537–566.

LAL, H., & LINDSLEY, O. R. Therapy of chronic constipation in a young child by rearranging social contingencies. *Behaviour Research and Therapy,* 1968, *6,* 484–485.

LANG, P. J. Fear reduction and fear behavior: Problems in treating a construct. In J. M. Schlien (Ed.), *Research in psychotherapy.* Vol. III. Washington, D.C.: American Psychological Association, 1968. Pp. 90–102.

LANG, P. J., & MELAMED, B. Case report: Avoidance conditioning therapy of an infant with chronic ruminative vomiting. *Journal of Abnormal Psychology,* 1969, *74,* 1–8.

LANG, P. J., MELAMED, B. G., & HART, J. A psychophysiological analysis of fear modification using automated desensitization procedure. *Journal of Abnormal Psychology*, 1970, *76*, 220–235.

LAZARUS, A. A. The results of behaviour therapy in 126 cases of severe neurosis. *Behaviour Research and Therapy*, 1963, *1*, 69–79.

LEMERE, F., & VOEGTLIN, W. An evaluation of the aversion treatment of alcoholism. *Quarterly Journal of Studies on Alcohol*, 1950, *11*, 199–204.

LICHTENSTEIN, E., HARRIS, D., BIRCHLER, G., WAHL, J., & SCHMAHL, D. Comparison of rapid smoking, warm, smoky air, and attention placebo in the modification of smoking behavior. *Journal of Consulting and Clinical Psychology*, 1973, *40*, 92–98.

LICK, J. M., & BOOTZIN, R. Covert sensitization for the treatment of obesity. Paper presented at the Annual Meeting of the Midwestern Psychological Association, Detroit, 1971.

LICK, J. R. Expectancy, false GSR feedback, and systematic desensitization in the modification of phobic behavior. *Journal of Consulting and Clinical Psychology*, in press.

LICK, J. R., & BOOTZIN, R. Expectancy factors in the treatment of fear: Methodological and theoretical issues. *Psychological Bulletin*, in press.

LOVAAS, O. I. Some studies on the treatment of childhood schizophrenia. In J. M. Schlien (Ed.), *Research in psychotherapy*. Vol. III. Washington, D.C.: American Psychological Association, 1968 Pp. 103–129.

LOVAAS, O. I., BERBERICH, J. P., PERLOFF, B. F., & SCHAEFFER, B. Acquisition of imitative speech by schizophrenic children. *Science*, 1966, *151*, 705–707.

LOVAAS, O. I., KOEGEL, R., SIMMONS, J. Q., & LONG, J. S. Some generalization and follow-up measures on autistic children in behavior therapy. *Journal of Applied Behavior Analysis*, 1973, *6*, 131–165.

MADSEN, C. H., JR., BECKER, W. C., THOMAS, D. R., KOSER, L., & PLAGER, E. An analysis of the reinforcing function of "sit down" commands. In R. K. Parker (Ed.), *Readings in educational psychology*. Boston: Allyn & Bacon, 1968. Pp. 265–278.

MAHONEY, M. J. *Cognition and behavior modification*. Cambridge, Mass.: Ballinger, 1974.

MAHONEY, M. J., MOURA, N. G. M., & WADE, T. C. The relative efficacy of self-reward, self-punishment, and self-monitoring techniques for weight loss. *Journal of Consulting and Clinical Psychology*, 1973, *40*, 404–407.

MALETZKY, B. "Assisted" covert sensitization in the treatment of exhibitionism. *Journal of Consulting and Clinical Psychology*, 1974, *42*, 34–40.

MARCIA, J. E., RUBIN, B. M., & EFRAN, J. S. Systematic desensitization: Expectancy change or counterconditioning? *Journal of Abnormal Psychology*, 1969, *74*, 382–387.

MARKS, I. M., & GELDER, M. G. Transvestism and fetishism: Clinical and psychological changes during faradic aversion. *British Journal of Psychiatry*, 1967, *119*, 711–730.

McFALL, R., & MARSTON, A. An experimental investigation of behavior rehearsal in assertive training. *Journal of Abnormal Psychology*, 1970, *76*, 295–303.

McFALL, R. M., & TWENTYMAN, C. T. Four experiments on the relative contributions of rehearsal, modeling and coaching to assertion training. *Journal of Abnormal Psychology*, 1973, *81*(3), 199–218.

McMICHAEL, J. S., & COREY, J. R. Contingency management in an introductory psychology course produces better learning. *Journal of Applied Behavior Analysis*, 1969, *2*, 79–83.

MEICHENBAUM, D. Examination of model characteristics in reducing avoidance behavior. *Journal of Personality and Social Psychology*, 1971, *17*, 298–307.

MEICHENBAUM, D. Self-instructional methods. In F. Kanfer and A. Goldstein (Eds.), *Helping people change*. New York: Pergamon, 1975.

MEICHENBAUM, D., & CAMERON, R. Training schizophrenics to talk to themselves: A means of developing attentional controls. *Behavior Therapy*, 1973, *4*, 515–534.

MELAMED, B., & LANG, P. J. Study of the automated desensitization of fear. Paper presented at the Annual Meeting of the Midwestern Psychological Association, Chicago, 1967.

MILLER, S. B. The contribution of therapeutic instructions to systematic desensitization. *Behaviour Research and Therapy*, 1972, *10*, 159–170.

MILLS, K. C., SOBELL, M. B., & SCHAEFER, H. H. Training social drinking as an alternative to abstinence for alcoholics. *Behavior Therapy*, 1971, *2*, 18–27.

MURPHY, C. M., & BOOTZIN, R. R. Active and passive participation in the contact desensitization of snake fear in children. *Behavior Therapy*, 1973, *4*, 203–211.

NICASSIO, P., & BOOTZIN, R. A comparison of progressive relaxation and autogenic training as treatments for insomnia. *Journal of Abnormal Psychology*, 1974, *83*(3), 253–260.

O'LEARY, K. D., & BECKER, W. C. The effects of the intensity of a teacher's reprimands on children's behavior. *Journal of School Psychology*, 1968, *7*, 8–11.

OLIVEAU, D. C., AGRAS, W. S., LEITENBERG, H., MOORE, R. C., &

WRIGHT, D. E. Systematic desensitization, therapeutically oriented instructions and selective positive reinforcement. *Behaviour Research and Therapy,* 1969, 7, 27–33.

PATTERSON, G. R. *Families: Applications of social learning to family life.* Champaign, Ill.: Research Press, 1971.

PATTERSON, G. R. Interventions for boys with conduct problems: Multiple settings, treatments, and criteria. *Journal of Consulting and Clinical Psychology,* 1974, 42, 471–481.

PATTERSON, G. R., & BRODSKY, G. A behavior modification programme for a child with multiple problem behaviors. *Journal of Child Psychology and Psychiatry,* 1966, 7, 277–295.

PATTERSON, G. R., & GUILLION, M. D. *Living with children: New methods for parents and teachers.* Champaign, Ill.: Research Press, 1968.

PAUL, G. L. *Insight vs. desensitization in psychotherapy: An experiment in anxiety reduction.* Stanford, Calif.: Stanford University Press, 1966.

PAUL, G. L. Outcome of systematic desensitization: I. Background procedures, and uncontrolled reports of individual treatment. In C. M. Franks (Ed.), *Behavior therapy: Appraisal and status.* New York: McGraw-Hill, 1969a.

PAUL, G. L. Outcome of systematic desensitization: II. Controlled investigations of individual treatment, technique variations, and current status. In C. M. Franks (Ed.), *Behavior therapy: Appraisal and status.* New York: McGraw-Hill, 1969b.

POWELL, J., & AZRIN, N. The effects of shock as a punisher for cigarette smoking. *Journal of Applied Behavior Analysis,* 1968, 1, 63–71.

PREMACK, D. Reinforcement theory. In D. Levine (Ed.), *Nebraska Symposium on Motivation: 1965.* Lincoln: University of Nebraska Press, 1965. Pp. 123–180.

RACHMAN, S., MARKS, I., & HODGSON, R. The treatment of obsessive-compulsive neurotics by modeling and flooding *in vivo. Behaviour Research and Therapy,* 1973, 11, 463–471.

RACHMAN, S., & TEASDALE, J. *Aversion therapy and behaviour disorders: An analysis.* Coral Gables: University of Miami Press, 1969.

READ, G. *Childbirth without fear—the principles and practice of natural childbirth.* New York: Harper & Row, 1959.

RITTER, B. The group treatment of children's snake phobias using vicarious and contact desensitization procedures. *Behaviour Research and Therapy,* 1968, 6, 1–6.

RITTER, B. The use of contact desensitization, demonstration-plus-participation, and demonstration alone in the treatment of acrophobia. *Behaviour Research and Therapy,* 1969, 7, 157–164.

RUTNER, I., & BUGLE, C. An experimental procedure for the modification of psychotic behavior. *Journal of Consulting and Clinical Psychology,* 1969, *33,* 651–653.

SAJWAJ, T., LIBET, J. & AGRAS, W. S. Lemon-juice therapy: The control of life-threatening rumination in a 6-month-old infant. *Journal of Applied Behavior Analysis,* 1974, *7,* 557–567.

SALTER, A. *Conditioned reflex therapy.* New York: Capricorn Books, 1949.

SCHAEFER, H. H. Twelve-month follow-up of behaviorally trained ex-alcoholic social drinkers. *Behavior Therapy,* 1972, *3,* 286–289.

SCHMAHL, D., LICHTENSTEIN, E., & HARRIS, D. Successful treatment of habitual smokers with warm, smoky air and rapid smoking. *Journal of Consulting and Clinical Psychology,* 1972, *38,* 105–111.

SCHULTZ, J. H., & LUTHE, W. *Autogenic training.* New York: Grune & Stratton, 1959.

SHERMAN, J. A., & BAER, D. M. Appraisal of operant therapy techniques with children and adults. In C. M. Franks (Ed.), *Behavior therapy: Appraisal and status.* New York: McGraw-Hill, 1969. Pp. 192–219.

SKINNER, B. F. *Walden II.* New York: Macmillan, 1948.

SKINNER, B. F. *Beyond freedom and dignity.* New York: Knopf, 1971.

SOBELL, M., & SOBELL, L. Individualized behavior therapy for alcoholics. *Behavior Therapy,* 1973a, *4,* 49–72.

SOBELL, M., & SOBELL, L. Alcoholics treated by individualized behavior therapy: One year treatment outcome. *Behaviour Research and Therapy,* 1973b, *11,* 599–619.

SOLOMON, R. L. Punishment. *American Psychologist,* 1964, *19,* 239–253.

SOLOMON, R. L., KAMIN, L. J., & WYNNE, L. C. Traumatic avoidance learning: The outcomes of several extinction procedures with dogs. *Journal of Abnormal and Social Psychology,* 1953, *48,* 291–302.

SOLOMON, R. L., & WYNNE, L. C. Traumatic avoidance learning: Acquisition in normal dogs. *Psychological Monographs,* 1953, *67,* No. 4 (Whole No. 354).

STAATS, A. W., MINKE, K. A., FINLEY, J. R., WOLF, M. M., & BROOKS, L. O. A reinforcer system and experimental procedure for the laboratory study of reading acquisition. *Child Development,* 1964, *35,* 209–231.

STAMPFL, T. G., & LEVIS, D. J. Essentials of implosive therapy: A learning-theory-based psychodynamic behavioral therapy. *Journal of Abnormal Psychology,* 1967, *72,* 496–503.

STUART, R. B. Behavioral control of overeating. *Behaviour Research and Therapy,* 1967, *5,* 357–365.

STUART, R. Behavioral contracting with the families of delinquents. *Journal of Behavior Therapy and Experimental Psychiatry,* 1971, *2,* 1–11.

STUART, R., & DAVIS, B. *Slim chance in a fat world: Behavioral control of obesity.* Champaign, Ill.: Research Press, 1972.

SZASZ, T. S. *Law, liberty and psychiatry.* New York: Macmillan, 1963.

ULLMANN, L. P., & KRASNER, L. *Case studies in behavior modification.* New York: Holt, Rinehart and Winston, 1965. Pp. 1–65.

ULRICH, R., STACHNIK, T., & MABRY, J. (Eds.) *Control of human behavior.* Vols. I and II. Glenview, Ill.: Scott, Foresman, 1966, 1970.

VOEGTLIN, W. L., LEMERE, F., & BROZ, W. R. Conditioned reflex therapy of alcoholic addiction: III. An evaluation of present results in the light of previous experiences with this method. *Quarterly Journal of Studies on Alcohol,* 1940, *1,* 501–516.

WATSON, J. B., & RAYNER, R. Conditioned emotional reactions. *Journal of Experimental Psychology,* 1920, *3,* 1–14.

WEISSBROD, C., & BRYAN, J. Film treatment as an effective fear reduction technique. *Journal of Abnormal Child Psychology,* 1973, *1,* 196–201.

WEXLER, D. B. Token and taboo: Behavior modification, token economies, and the law. *Behaviorism: A forum for critical discussion,* 1973, *1,* 1–24. Reprinted from *California Law Review,* 1973, *61,* 81–109.

WOLF, M. M., RISLEY, T., & MEES, H. L. Application of operant conditioning procedures to the behaviour problems of an autistic child. *Behaviour Research and Therapy,* 1964, *1,* 305–312.

WOLPE, J. *The practice of behavior therapy,* 2d ed. New York: Pergamon, 1973.

WOLPE, J. *Psychotherapy by reciprocal inhibition.* Stanford, Calif.: Stanford University Press, 1958.

WOLPE, J., & LAZARUS, A. A. *Behavior therapy techniques.* New York: Pergamon, 1966.

Wyatt v. Stickney, 344 F. Supp. 373 (M.D. Ala. 1972).

ZEISSET, R. M. Desensitization and relaxation in the modification of psychiatric patients' interview behavior. *Journal of Abnormal Psychology,* 1968, *73,* 18–24.

Author Index

173

Subject Index